LET
GOD

The Transforming Wisdom of
François Fénelon

Winn Collier

Dirty Paper *Press*

Let God: The Transforming Wisdom of François Fénelon

2007 First Printing, 2017 Second Printing

ISBN: 978-0-69285-770-0

Published by Dirty Paper Press
Charlottesville, VA
www.winncollier.com

Printed in the United States of America

To Mom and Dad,
God graciously gave you to me as my
very first guides.
I love you.

Contents

Contents

Preface

Preface

My days spent with Fénelon on this project have been both pleasurable and unnerving. The time has been pleasurable because I have enjoyed hours with a man who is wise and kind and who has just the right type of authority (strong, yet never harsh). It has been unnerving because, as I've worked, I've had this nagging question of whether or not Fénelon would like the way I've modernized his message. The funny thing is that I think Fénelon would be more concerned by the self-obsession of the question than by any of the blunders of the text (and no doubt there are blunders). "Let it go. Trust," I hear Fénelon saying. "It's not up to you to get it right."

So, I will try.

Fénelon's original French work has been well-preserved, but not all of it has been translated into English. This book is comprised primarily from a collection of Fénelon's correspondence translated into English by M.W. Dodd in 1853 entitled *Spiritual Letters*.[1]

I have put these letters together thematically, taking into account some of the obvious questions and issues Fénelon responded to with his friends. We have little record of the letters precipitating Fénelon's replies. We don't know the names of those to whom he wrote. However, recently I was in a university library and found Fénelon's multivolume French collection among the musty lower-level stacks. I opened it to find pictures of actual letters, with Fénelon's elegant scrawl. Something about seeing pen strokes instead of crisp, typed letters made it all more real. These were real people writing one another, sharing hope and disappointment, sin and joy.[2]

My work is a paraphrase, not a translation. I want Fénelon's voice to be heard in a fresh way. I hope to allow Fénelon's words to breathe again, in a new time and place. But I hope I have not meddled with Fénelon's essence. Part of Fénelon's appeal for me is that he is a voice with authority, a voice that can be trusted to tell me the truth, even if the truth is hard.

While Fénelon's wisdom is timeless, his syntax and idiom and metaphor are not. What's more, Fénelon wrote letters, not treatises. His sentences helped foster a relationship to enjoy, not just a theological principle to follow. I believe it honors Fénelon and Fénelon's way to nudge these old words back to where they began, to a place of warm, plainspoken friendship.

This is why even the word *paraphrase* falls a bit flat. I've thought of this work more as a conversation. I have listened to Fénelon and then seen what his words and wisdom have evoked in me, where they have pricked and challenged, where they have unleashed hope and life. I hope you will be able to have this same sort of experience. The original context of these words was in conversation, so I think Fénelon would be pleased for us to enjoy the same relational dialogue. Fénelon loved to chat. Let him chat with you on these pages.

Introduction

Fénelon's Voice to Guide Us

Miska handed me back the ring. It was the hardest thing I'd ever done, reaching out and taking it back. But I didn't think I had a choice. Just a few days earlier, I'd asked Miska to marry me. We were on top of a mountain in the Rockies, and the stars were out. It was gorgeous, just the way I'd planned, the last thing that went as planned. Miska said yes. We kissed. And then something snapped in my head. Fear landed on me like a baby grand piano tossed onto my head from a few stories up. I descended into a gloom I couldn't pull out of. A few days later, I owned both the fear and the ring.

A month later, I was still reeling. My plan was to give myself some more time, to figure out what was rattling around in my head and why this vise grip had locked down on my heart. Truthfully, I was lost. I thought I loved Miska. I was sure I wanted to get married. So what was going on? I figured more time would cure my panic—at least that's what I was counting on.

Then I had a conversation that changed my life. I met with an older man to talk about some other issues I was facing. I don't think that I planned for the conversation to center on my botched engagement. But it did. With little small talk, he moved us right there. He didn't have much to say, really. No big words or amazing psychological insights. He didn't impart any mystic spiritual wisdom. What he said was this: "Winn, it's time to be a man." He told me to make a decision. Now. To stop dangling Miska along. To figure out what I wanted. And to move.

I did. That night, a man on a mission, I drove six hours to her house and got down on my knee a second time and asked her if she would marry me. She said yes, and my world was forever changed. Because a wiser, older man had stepped into my life.

Many of us live with questions, wondering if anyone will step into our life. Who will guide us when we face complexities and questions and myriads of choices? Who will help us when fear or shame or lethargy descends on our hearts? Who will tell us we will be okay when it seems that everything we know has crumbled? Who will have the courage to tell us we are wrong when we have deluded ourselves into believing just the opposite? Who will instruct us in matters of the soul? Who will help us become the woman or the man God intends for us to be?

Friends are good in such times, and we would each do well to have two or three soul friends who enter into such places with us. However, a friend is not always what we need; even a deep one will not always do. We need someone who is more weathered than us, someone whose courage has been tested and whose wisdom carries a certain moxie. We need someone unflustered by our circumstances, unimpressed with our hubris, unafraid of our vileness. We need someone who speaks with gravity, whose words are simple and straight and true. We need someone with authority.

Our hearts ache for a woman or man, older and wiser, to speak strong words of hope and life, for the wisdom that comes only with many long years lived in the way of Jesus.

I have recently been in conversation with two friends, each a man who is trying to figure out who he is and what he is about. Both of them said the same thing: "I want someone to tell me what to do." Whether we face chaos and darkness or are merely attempting the lifelong process of following Jesus in our world, there are times when we need the voice of someone whose life and age and wisdom insist we be quiet and listen. I believe this to be a human constant. We need guides. Old or young, woman or man, we are all the same. And, eventually, most of us come to this conclusion: a spiritual life is not something we can do on our own.

But sadly, many of us are alone, and we don't know where to turn. I have an early memory. I was young, perhaps three. Apparently, there are certain traumas that lodge themselves in a young psyche and won't let go. My parents and I were in a K-Mart, where I vaguely remember some voice announcing a Blue-Light Special being offered among the labyrinth of shopping aisles. Something must have grabbed my attention, and I darted off, slipping away from my parents and into the exhilarating world of potential playthings. Soon, however, what was adventurous and enticing grew menacing and frightful. I realized I was alone. It was a new, terrifying experience to fling at a three-year-old soul. I don't know how long I stood there in panic, but now, in this terrifying place, I didn't know what to do. All I had were fear and questions. All I had was myself.

Thankfully, two attentive nuns noticed a very frightened young boy. They kindly came up beside me, stooped down, asked my name, and told me I would be okay. They took me to the customer service counter, where a crackling voice hit the PA system, letting the entire store know that there was a little boy waiting for his parents. Within moments, Mom and Dad arrived and gathered me up. I was safe. I was home. Yet I had needed a guide—in this instance, two guides—to show me the way.

I am no longer a little boy, but I still need guides. One I have found is named François Fénelon. A French bishop who lived from 1651 until 1715, Fénelon lived and served during tumultuous times. Louis XIV sat on the French throne, and his court was notorious for its debased character. Louis' reign was characterized by lust for power, copious extravagance, and sexual perversions. Fénelon was intimately acquainted with both the lure and the repulsion of Louis' influence. He served for a time as the tutor for the king's grandson, the heir to the throne. Later, when Fénelon served a spiritual community farther away from the royal trappings, he continued to offer spiritual guidance for a number of younger friends still serving in Louis' court. Fénelon offered his wisdom to these young Christians most often through correspondence. He would write them letters, answering their questions, challenging their assumptions, guiding them in matters of the soul. Thankfully, many of these letters are preserved for us today.

There are a number of collections of Fénelon's correspondence, but one that has particular merit is a collection pieced together and translated into English in 1853. It was titled *Spiritual Letters,* and through these words of wisdom and direction, I found Fénelon becoming one of my guides. Words on a page from a voice long passed will never replace the immediate presence of a flesh-and-blood sage. However, Fénelon's voice—

preserved for us centuries later—is remarkably relevant. These words offer us a voice some of us might never hear otherwise.

Much of the power of Fénelon's voice is due to the form in which it comes. The fact that we are reading letters is central to how we must hear them. These are personal letters to particular people with urgent needs and questions. Fénelon is not waxing eloquent on theoretical maxims removed from pain or bewilderment or sin or shame. Fénelon has walked into the deep waters of fear and loneliness and disillusionment and regret. And he is holding out his hand, telling us to trust and to follow him and his Jesus forward. As I read Fénelon, I wish I had a contemporary guide like him, gifted for this unique spiritual direction, who is simply a letter or a phone call or an e-mail away. But even while I hope for such guides, I do have Fénelon. The world he speaks to is not so different from my own. The young pilgrims he guides are certainly little different from me. In Fénelon, we each can have a guide . . . if we will hear him.

I am most intrigued with the context in which Fénelon writes. Most of his young friends were situated in the middle of a place where sin and power reigned. Their world was steeped in power grabs and self-promotion and a commitment to giving one's self to any whim or passing desire that might shuffle by. Notions of peace and discipline and sacrifice and mercy were entirely out of favor, almost unknown. How would these correspondents love and obey Jesus in the midst of such depravity? This question and the culture that forced it form the background to Fénelon's letters. Though he rarely refers to such realities overtly, it is the steady milieu in which he writes. He encourages a tribe of young disciples to seek a subversive and radical life of incarnation. He never encourages them to do the easy thing and withdraw from the darkness surrounding them. Rather, he encourages them to, like Jesus who came as God in the flesh, incarnate a new way in the very middle of the old way. Fénelon prods his correspondents toward the improbable. He suggests that they subvert the lies by simply living the truth.

Many of us long for a wise elder voice to provide us with spiritual direction. We do not want to be coddled or cajoled. We do not want to be given small-minded moralisms. We long for depth and authenticity. We do not want a quick fix or a trite answer. We just want a wiser voice, one who knows God and his ways. And we want to learn how to live in our world in a manner that is truly good. If we will listen to Fénelon, we will find much of what we seek.

First Conversation
Why Is God So Peculiar?

It is a stark truth when we first run up against it:

God isn't always the safe bet or the sure thing.

God disappoints us, and this disappointment

can be the bitterest kind. It often comes in

those tender places where our hearts

are most vulnerable or most hopeful

or most desperate. We believe

God will act for us, and

sometimes . . . we hear

nothing.

Our disorientation is understandable; we seem set up for it. Often, when we come to faith, it is because we need protection. We need protection from our sin, from ourselves, from loneliness or despair, from all the assaults on our heart and our soul. These are primal needs, and they draw us to God because we realize that we are helpless on our own. It is easy then to see that early in our spiritual journey, we can succumb to the temptation to believe that God is the one who makes everything right, all the time, in the manner and at the moment we require. There is some truth here. Scripture is so bold as to tell us that God will not disappoint us. But he does. How do we make sense of this?

Spiritual guides of most every century have attempted to tell us this truth: there is a difference between what we think God should do for us and what God actually does for us. There is a difference between whom we imagine God to be and who God actually is. Becoming a follower of God is hard because it requires that we submit ourselves fully to a God who is other than us. We must let go of our insistence that we know best what we need. We must let go of our demands that God act when and how we demand.

With each letting go, we release layers of our self-protection. This self-protection is our futile attempt to manage life. It's the same seductive force pushing at us to attempt to manage God. But God won't leave us to wallow there. He will help us, but he must upset our addiction to control. He will have to unravel all the demands we have placed on him. This is why God's disappointment is necessary. He is helping us, peeling back our fingers, loosening our white-knuckled grip from our life. He has to; if we will ever be free in his care, he has to.

Free in God's care—that's where we're headed. But we aren't there yet. It will take a lifetime to get us there. For now, there are days when prayers are unanswered or when hopes go unfulfilled. Jobs don't pan out. Relationships fall apart. Mentors and friends and spouses may leave us empty. God may seem silent. Sometimes he moves in ways we would never have imagined, and his movement leaves us breathless with thankfulness and joy. At other times, we will be just sure God is going to set things right or intervene or show us a way out of our suffering. He doesn't, though, and God's unpredictability leaves us bewildered.

God is peculiar, Fénelon would say. And I think these peculiar patches in the soul are where Fénelon has some of his best wisdom to offer. He has great hope that God—in the end—will not disappoint us, because, in the end, God has given us his full self. The path takes strange bends, though. God moves in strange, peculiar ways. We desperately need wise spiritual guides to point out the way, to tell us to keep moving, to put a hand on our shoulder and tell us that the darkness will not consume us, to tell us that God's peculiar ways are signals of grace, and that we must just wait and see.

WINN COLLIER

To a Friend Facing God's Hard Mercy

Dear friend,

It might not seem obvious to you, but I am convinced that God is treating you as one of his friends. It's plain as day. God's friendship is obvious as he hands you crosses, provides you with space to suffer, and offers you opportunities, even to squander your self-honor—if you wish it. It will be hard, but is a *good* hard. The suffering will draw you into God. Are you up for it?

The means that God initiates to draw a soul to himself burrow in and do a much quicker and more skillful work than any effort we would attempt of our own devising. God slices self-love at its very root. However, for all our work and self-discipline, we would never be able to dig as far as God. God knows all the ways our self-love winds and hides, and God attacks it even where it has dug in the deepest.

If we had strength and faith enough to trust that God would take care of us, and if we were brave enough to follow God wherever he would want to lead us, we would have no need to exert great mental energy in order to grow in faith. However, our faith is weak, and we are convinced we have to know all the answers from God before we launch out on the journey. This makes our road longer and our spiritual transformation slower.

Abandon yourself entirely to God. Recklessly abandon yourself to God as long as you breathe on this earth. Let loose. You are in good hands. You can be self-abandoned because you will never be God-abandoned.

To a Friend Finding Hope in Humility

Dear friend,

Often, I pray to God that he will hold you near him, with tender strength. That is what I pray that God will do. This is what I pray that *you* will do: I pray that you will be courageous enough to willingly walk the hard way, the way of humility. Humility is the most essential thing for you right now. This submissive path you must take will actually help you with the wide range of difficulties you face. The journey, if you allow it, will teach you willingness to learn and to listen. Even better, this willingness to humbly receive what God has to teach you will eventually smooth out your rough road. If you choose to resist God (which is the same as resisting humility), you will bear more blame than a lot of other people who have never faced the challenges you have faced. These challenges are a gift, an invitation into a deep journey. Don't squander it.

On the one hand, you have received large doses of light and grace. The truth has been illuminated to you. Now become humble with your fresh-lit truth, like a little child. On the other hand, no one else has experienced what you have. Hard and distressing experiences hurl you into churning, chaotic waters. As you desperately splash around and fight to stay afloat, you surrender to the humble truth that you need help. The rough, humbling waters have wrecked your self-confidence.

And this is good. There is hope in the humility we find on a hard path and in rough waters.

Whenever our weakness is so obvious that we cannot deny it, we might think we are bankrupt. Oddly, however, we are on the cusp of amazing profit if we allow this weakness to make us humble and obedient. I pray the Lord will hold you and love you exactly where you are!

To a Delightfully Impoverished Friend

Dear friend,

Everything in your life plays its part in uncovering the true identity of your soul. However, there is no need to fear that you will be taken under. The God who loves you will not allow your temptations to have more muscle than the strength you have to face them. God will use your hardship to elbow you forward.

But we must not look obsessively inward, forever curious to see how well we are progressing, or how much our spiritual stamina is growing. We shouldn't even give much energy toward trying to see precisely how God is working in us. You won't be able to see much anyway—most of God's work is invisible. But don't worry; invisibility doesn't make it any less potent. God works best (and most often) in secret.

We would never get over ourselves if God always worked out in the open where we could always see him, with God always bringing some grand miracle to our rescue. It is difficult for God to do a good work if he is limited to working only in broad daylight. It is difficult for God to do a good work if he is limited to using only what is comfortable or easy or obvious.

We will not always be aware of what God is up to. We will not always have a firm grasp on our life and what God is crafting of it. We are going to have to let it loose. Letting loose will allow us to follow God into these shadow places. To follow God, we must walk into the cross, and to walk into the cross is to walk into darkness and poverty, nakedness and death.

In the Gospel of Matthew, Christ did not say, *If anyone wants to follow me, all he needs to do is enjoy himself and be drunk with everything he thinks he wants and feel smug satisfaction over how perfect he is.* Christ did not say, *If anyone wants to follow me, all she needs to do is perfect her image and be forever looking at herself in the mirror to make sure she has everything together.* Quite the opposite, Jesus' words are: *If anyone wants to follow me, I will show them the road they must take. All they need to do is say no to themselves. Next they can pick up their cross. And after they have done these two things, they can follow me along a path that will take them perilously close to dangerous precipices. They will see nothing but death all around them.*

How is that? What does that do to our thought that God should always keep us safe from temptation and danger? The apostle Paul talks about the strong human desire to be clothed well, to be snug and safe. However, the truth is that we need to be stripped naked. Then, when we are naked, Christ can finally be our clothes, our protection, our comfort.

Give way to God. Surrender. Allow him to wreck the beautiful self-image you have spent so much time creating. Let God dig into the most hidden corner of your heart where this self-obsession lurks. Jesus died on a cross because you are dirty and sinful—your filthiness, your lack, is no surprise to him. But God wants to clean away your filth, and then to fill you up with goodness. Let him. It might not seem like it, but this is a wonderful thing when you have nothing, when you are impoverished. Feel the joy of having nothing, absolutely nothing. Feel the joy of being entirely at Jesus' mercy. Feel the alive pleasure of no longer clinging to your own so-called beauty, but hoping deeply in (and for) the beauty of Jesus.

God's romance is peculiar, requiring us to go against our instincts. We give everything we are and have to God; we give way to complete poverty. Yet, even as we do what seems foolish, we find God being amazingly generous, filling us back up. God holds nothing back; God gives us all of himself. We are then every bit as beautiful as God is. We are then just as full as God is full. God's love will drown us then because—and I told you this was strange—God will be loving himself. God will have taken away all our ugliness and will have filled us with his beauty—and God finds his beauty immensely attractive.

Listen to me with this. Believe it. I know that when you taste this truth, it will seem bitter, but if you will hear it, it will feed your heart well. You will need to die to yourself, the ultimate impoverishment. But this death is the only true life, the only way to be filled. Trust what I am saying. Don't listen to your self-protective voice. That voice is the grand seducer, more powerful even than the serpent that deceived our mother Eve. That voice coddles you into being afraid to risk what God requires. Trust me: you will find happiness if you simply listen to and obey the *other* voice.

To a Friend Under God's Knife

Dear friend,

We think our eagerness to serve others is always a noble thing. Unfortunately, too often it actually surges from only natural inclinations of human generosity. Worse is when our supposed generosity actually spurts from a polished-up version of plain selfishness, where we gain something (like a good image or a good dose of self-righteousness) from the transaction. If this is the case, we will often find ourselves eventually disdaining those we are serving or simply growing spent and frustrated with the whole thing. However, true charity is simple. It stays steady, always offering the same genuineness, the same love, towards our neighbor. True love gives itself away, stays humble, and ignores all the selfishness that obstructs its flow. Anything that isn't this kind of love—simple love—well, cut it off.

This is the way God works, always has: God had Abraham and all who followed him do the cutting work of circumcision to symbolize the work God was doing in them. Now, God still does this same kind of cutting; only now it's invisible to the human eye. God does what Scripture calls a "circumcision of the heart." He makes us his children, giving us all of his care. And, again like Abraham, God asks us to trust him, to follow without having to know all the details about where we are heading or how we are going to make the trip. It won't seem like it, but letting God cut away at us is a good thing.

We cannot cut that deep—even Abraham could cut only what was on the outside, never the heart. We don't know what we need. We have no idea what in us most needs to be sliced. Left to ourselves, we would not be able to find or reach the exact spot that needs the swift knife, but God, knife in hand, goes right to it.

We are too infatuated with ourselves, and we don't care much for pain. So if the cutting were up to us, we would always pull our hand back. We would never let the knife pierce where it must. We don't have the courage to wound ourselves in the truly deep place, where the pain will be severe, but God doesn't hold back. God has the courage. He will cut in unexpected places, where we never would. God's stab goes deep, and it leaves nothing untouched that needs his knife. God is the surgeon, and our self-absorption is the cancer. God's knife will hurt, and so it is okay to cry out in pain. However, we must make sure we do not squirm out from under God's steady, skilled hand as it moves in with the scalpel. If we fight too much, God's surgery will not be able to do all that is necessary. As we remain still under the knife, we need to do only one thing: receive every cut, every single one.

I admire John the Baptist. He forgot all about himself, and he gave all his attention to Christ. He pointed to Christ. He was a lone voice crying in the wilderness. John's one purpose was to prepare people for Jesus' coming. He even sent Jesus all his own disciples. It wasn't so much John the Baptist's quirky and ascetic life (like living in the woods, eating locusts, and wearing camel-hair clothes) that made him a great man, a powerful prophet. No, his greatness came through the way he lived, the way he gave his entire self to Jesus. John couldn't possibly have imagined how God wanted to speak through him. John's only concern was to obey God, to say what God wanted him to say, peculiar as it must have seemed.

John obeyed. And God spoke.

To a Friend Finding Happiness in Suffering

Dear friend,

I want you to know how deeply sorry I am for all your unhappiness. This life is a time of living between: between God's promises and God's making those promises reality. In the between, then, we must carry the cross. There is much hope, though. Soon, we won't suffer at all. When we are living in (and watching over) God's kingdom, we will have joy, not sadness. God's fingers will wipe away our tears. When you are with the God of all pleasure, pain and wishing for more won't exist. This delight is what is ahead for you. The sorrow and hardness you face now is only a blip on the broad timeline of your life.

However, it would be a huge mistake to miss what God has for you *now*, in this place. It would be easy in your suffering to miss how valuable the cross (and even your suffering) actually is. But it is more valuable than you could imagine—don't lose one thing this cross of suffering longs to teach you. It is hard, yes. Something far better is ahead for you, absolutely. But this hard place now also offers you God.

Here's something to help now: when you suffer, do it humbly and in peace. We have a tendency to exaggerate our difficulties, to make them appear worse than they actually are. We can even play them out in our mind, letting our imagination gallop off, making the whole experience truly bigger than life. Just suffer simply. When we take the simple route, without all the selfish drama, it makes the suffering smaller. It's like carrying only half a cross. If we are able to suffer simply, fully aware of love, we will find happiness. Here is the wildest part: our happiness will not be *in spite* of our cross, but *because* of it.

True love finds pleasure when it is giving to, suffering for, someone it deeply loves; and we are suffering for God. This cross and this suffering make us more like God. Deep pleasure and intimacy come from being bonded to God in this way.

Second Conversation

How Do I Pursue Spiritual Maturity?

How do we grow up?

For any of us who want to become more serious in our

faith or more committed to the way of Jesus, this is

the question we inevitably ask. Our attempts to

answer the question have even spawned an

entire mega-industry of propaganda and

merchandise. As with fad diets, we can

spend an entire life hopping from one

promised fix to the next: a highly

touted experience. A seven-step

plan. A bracelet. A bumper

sticker. The next big

b o o k .

Fénelon invites us to choose another way. Fénelon suggests that the way of growing into spiritual maturity is far harder and far easier than all this. It is harder because we can't ingest maturity by popping a pill, gulping down words, or taking a weekend retreat. Books and experiences might help, but they aren't the "fix." No high-profile guru or slickly marketed system will manufacture maturity. It comes only when Jesus is allowed room to dig in and root around and do the slow, often painful work. It's hard, and it takes time.

Maturity is also easier than we might think, because the focus isn't on us. This is the problem with all faddish efforts. They often focus on our energy, our resilience, our discipline. All this self-focus is lethal to spiritual growth. It is like poison sprayed on fresh spring sprouts. It stops them, dead on the vine. Isn't it strange then that so many attempts at spiritual growth focus so much on us?

Left to ourselves, floundering amid all the spiritual debris, we feel hopeless. If these other paths are short-lived and doomed to disappoint, what do we do? We wait. We ratchet down all the nervous energy and the compulsion to get it all squared away. Now. Immediately. We wait, and we listen. And when God sends us that subversive guide, like "one crying in the wilderness," we then get up and follow.

Fénelon is such a voice. He is quiet, yet full of authority. He has such a different way. He doesn't offer a plan. He offers Jesus. To some friends, Fénelon advises they need to move. To other friends, he suggests they sit still. Some friends need to practice more obedience, while others need to stop trying so hard. The context for developing spiritual maturity is a relationship, not a laboratory. Our spiritual lives come of age through conversations and friendships, through stories told and heard, through learning who we are and how to listen to the God who best knows who we are. This is why we need a guide, not a method—because there is no single way to grow into Jesus.

WINN COLLIER

To a Friend in Pain

My dear daughter,

I have heard that you are very sick. I love you dearly, and I am suffering with you.

This might be hard to hear, but even though I feel strong compassion for your pain, I must kiss the hand that is afflicting you. In fact, I am going to ask you to also kiss this afflicting hand with tender thankfulness. The truth is that up to now, you have abused your health. You have disregarded the pleasure you should receive from caring for yourself. The sickness and pain you now experience are the natural result of a long season of abusing yourself.

This is my prayer for you: that God will weaken your self-obsessed spirit more than he weakens your body. I pray that God will give your body all the care and comfort it needs, but I also pray that God will entirely crush your internal addiction to self. We are actually just coming to a place of strength when we begin to see how weak and anemic we truly are. When we see our feebleness, then we can begin to see where we have run off course. We can begin to repent and change. We can actually receive wise, helpful words from others, words we were unwilling to hear before. We can stop thinking we have all the answers. We can abandon the foolish arrogance of assuming we always know what is best for ourselves.

When we see our weakness, we speak with simplicity and humility even when we are convinced we are speaking the truth. We don't get edgy when we are being corrected, and we don't flinch when someone points out some darkness in us. When we are weak—and know it—we don't feel the compulsion to hold onto so much. Even while we are open to being corrected by others, we are far less snappy to correct other people. We speak words of rebuke only if we absolutely must—and we offer hard words only to those who want to hear them. We simply speak what we think we see, but we aren't dogmatic about it. We know we could be wrong, and that's okay. Nothing is at stake for us—we aren't trying to hold onto our reputation, and we aren't trying to be the spiritual authority for everyone else. We don't care about being perceived as some wise spiritual sage. We just give what we have to give to whoever wants to receive it. It's pretty simple.

I pray for something else, too. I am praying that God will sit you down in a place where you are drinking in grace—and that God will hold you there and won't let you wiggle away. God has started a deep transformation in you, and I pray that he will continue. This is a good prayer; it's the same one the apostle Paul prayed in Philippians.

It isn't up to you, anyway; it's all up to God. We need to learn to be kind and patient and honest with ourselves. There's no need to flatter ourselves and try to talk ourselves into believing we're better than we are. There's nothing to hide, nothing to defend. At the same time, there's no need to lacerate ourselves. There's no need to hate our humanness and our weakness. God knows where we are and is working good in us. If we can allow ourselves to be where we are, right there with God, that very spot will be a place of transformation. We'll find we're in a place that's ready-made to renovate us with the subtle, powerful tenderness of grace.

But let this work happen quietly and peacefully. Don't rush into it, all fired up to get busy. Don't think God's transformation is going to happen in a day, and then you can get on with your life. Don't think about it too much. Don't try to figure it all out. Just move and obey and respond. With all the mental energy we exert, we can spend so much of our life hoarding knowledge that we will need another whole life to try to actually live any of it. We face the very real danger of thinking that our accumulation of "spiritual" knowledge is the indicator of our spiritual development. Not true.

Many of our spiritual truths and endless, glamorous spiritual theories actually get in the way. Rather than leading us into death of self, they actually foster more arrogant self-confidence. We love the learning, the knowledge, the illumination of ideas, just as Adam and Eve did in the Garden. But unfortunately, we do not love simply trusting, simply obeying, simply living.

So stop.

Stop trusting in your own mental or physical power. Stop trusting that you can figure God out or that you can manhandle your spiritual life, pushing and dragging it across some supposed finish line of maturity. If you just stop all the wrestling and resisting and harried effort, you will find yourself on your way to becoming who God has in mind for you to be.

I know you give lots of energy to all the heady or difficult virtues you think you should pursue. However, these are the virtues you really need: humility and self-distrust.

To a Friend in Need of Perspective

Dear friend,

I have a hope for you. I have a hope you will begin to experience the pervasive peace that comes into your life when you stop the pedantic scrutiny. Stop keeping track of how well you are doing. Stop living on high alert, trying to mark every inch of spiritual progress. That's enough to drive a person crazy.

I hope you will experience the calm that comes when you unplug your attempts to manage the complexities and the dangers you face. This is difficult, I know. We are addicted to protecting ourselves, but the notion that we can achieve anything of substance from our self-protection is an illusion. The illusion grows because we hold so much inside, secretly wrangling to control all that happens to us. If we will release control and let loose, the illusions won't have anywhere to work.

Here's how you can start releasing control: Be humble and simple, whether you are around the power brokers (the very sort of people that make you want to keep track of how well you are doing) or alone, with nobody to impress but yourself. Don't make any decision because it's what is expected or because it's what makes sense or because it just seems like it's what you want to do. That's illusion stuff. Rather, make every decision an act of listening to another voice: the Spirit of God. And then, after you've listened and heard, obey.

This Spirit speaks in a strange voice. It is a voice of life and death. This voice tells you to die to yourself (and to all the self-neurosis of keeping track and managing and protecting). But dying isn't the point; living is the main thing. The Spirit's voice tells you that life is found only in God. Don't be driven by manic excitement, where emotions run wild. Don't go on an obsessive inner search for absolute certainty, trying to make sure there is no possibility of making a mistake. Don't always be pining away for what might be better in the future, forgetting about today. God is your deep pleasure now, today.

Besides, in self-protection, you give yourself to smallness, and this smallness of yours will not magically grow to something larger or better off in the future. Small now, small later. If we count on some distant reality to somehow unravel all our struggles, we will be disappointed when we find our struggles just as twisted up then as they are today.

Let's live in today. Let's receive humbly whatever comes our way, not always wondering what more we could have, and not trying to hide the truth of smallness, of how selfish and afraid we are. Just let God be God.

God is at work; let him work. Abandon yourself fully to God, in this moment, in each day. Don't hold anything back. Don't worry about what will or won't be. Just be present, as though this very moment encompassed the whole of eternity.

To a Spiritually Exhausted Soul

Dear friend,

Ever since I read your letter yesterday, I've thought a lot about what you said. I have a growing confidence that God will take care of you. I know it's hard for you right now to enjoy any form of spiritual discipline. However, as much as you are able, continue to exercise your spiritual muscles. Someone sick won't have much of an appetite, but she still has to eat if she wants to live.

Here are a few simple things that I hope will do you good. Every once in a while, have a good conversation (and it doesn't have to be long) with those in your Christian community, those you can really trust with the hidden places of your soul. And don't worry, as I know you might, asking the frantic questions—*Who should I talk to?* and *How much should I say?* Just do what you want. If you want to talk, talk. The frantic stuff has nothing to do with God—that isn't how God works. You don't have to do a lot, just stay on the journey—that alone would make me happy.

Also, there is something very rich and pure about simply not giving up, particularly when there is little pleasure in your Christian experience. The truth is that you are actually in a better spiritual position when you aren't being governed by the whims of spiritual highs. All the giddy spiritual emotions can be something we work up, something we create out of our own desires.

Here's my additional advice: each day, read, just a little; and then spend time mediating, a little. It might not seem like much, but it will be the way God will give you enough wisdom and enough strength for what he will bring to you. If this still seems too hard, let's make it simple: just love God. I won't require you to do anything else.

The truth is, whatever else you need to do will grow from the soil of love. Even when I ask you to love, don't hear this as some heavy requirement to work up some emotional feeling of love. I know you may not have that in you right now. Just lean toward love. Just lean—you can do that. Of course, like everyone else, you have corruptness in your heart, but don't focus on that. Lean toward love, toward God. In this simple leaning, decide that what you want most is God—more than self and more than anything available in this world.

To a Friend Afraid of Dying

Dear friend,

It doesn't surprise me at all that the older you get and the more you feel your own mortality, the more you begin to think about dying. Me too. It's natural that as we get up in years, we think about death more. We can't help it. It's even more difficult given the fact that with increased age, there is often less to occupy our attention and distract our thoughts, but God uses even this. These fears feel like a burden, but they're a gift. God will use them to knock away our illusions about how gutsy and dead sure we are, convinced we can handle anything without breaking a sweat. God will use our burgeoning unease to allow us to face our weakness and to hold us firmly in a place of dependent humility. We will see what is true: that we are held up by God alone.

In these panicky times, God is able to make our sheer dependence blatant and obvious to us. Nothing gives us a good dose of our own vulnerability more than when our mind is running off without us. In the past we might have been doubt-free, owning a swagger in our certainty of God and God's ways. Now, the doubts run wild. No more swagger. We are scared, and we feel a vise-grip tightening on our soul.

This tight squeezing is a good thing, though. Humility requires this environment in order to work. Here, as we feel the weight of our weakness and our desperate need for God, the vise-grip presses even more, pushing all the toxins from our heart. The Scriptures repeatedly remind us that we aren't as good as we think we are: "No one living is righteous before you," the Psalms say; "Even the heavens are not pure in his eyes," Job tells us; and "We all stumble in many ways," says James.

In this vise-grip of our own mortality, we are able to see more of our weakness and a little less of our strength. This is good, because nothing helpful comes of staring too long at all our qualities we find so magnificent. Besides, when we ogle ourselves, we're mostly eyeballing a mirage. The image we interpret as burly is in truth usually puny. The image we interpret as gorgeous is in truth usually deformed.

Don't hesitate. Don't pause. Walk right into, right through, this fearful, stripping experience. Walk toward death the same way you have walked into every other spiritual exercise. Don't pull back just because fear is now in play. If we become aware of any sin or spiritual issue that needs correction, we should step into it. The same is true here with your concern about losing faith as death approaches.

Follow the light God is giving you. You do need to be careful here, though, because it might be easy to get overworked with introspection, consumed with small, meaningless things. Stay at peace. Don't listen to the voice of infatuation within yourself, wanting you to get all worked up and worried about dying. There's no reason to resist the inevitable. Death is inevitable. Instead, have a healthy detachment from life, the kind of recklessness that comes when you hand over all of yourself to God.

Solid confidence comes when you can shrug your shoulders, trust God, and keep strolling. When St. Ambrose was dying, someone asked him if he was afraid of God's judgments. "We have a good master," Ambrose said. This is what we need to tell ourselves: we need not fear death; we have a good God.

To die well, we don't just need a deep confidence of how God will judge us. We also need a deep confidence in our true identity; and our identity is God's gift to us. Our identity is not a do-it-yourself project we scrape together. Saint Augustine said that we need to be emptied of all we have tried to make of ourselves. That way, when we stand before God after death, we have only two things to give him: our utter brokenness **and** God's rich mercy. This is a brilliant way to arrive before God, because our brokenness is the very spot where he longs to pour his mercy—lots of it. And this overflowing mercy is the only thing that can ever make us (in any true sense) *good*.

So, whenever you are sad, read whatever will strengthen your confidence in God and firm up your heart. Read this from Psalm 73: "Surely God is good to Israel, to those who are pure in heart." Pray that you will have this kind of pure heart. God loves your passionate innocence, and when God encounters you with this heart-open faith, he can't help dumping compassion all over your sin and your failures.

To a Friend Surprised by God

Dear friend,

The person you wrote about in your letter sounds intriguing. I'm glad you found what you were looking for in your new friend. God acts in mysterious ways, doesn't he? We set limitations on how (or through whom) God needs to meet us. But God dismisses that silliness, walking right past our demands and using people we would never have expected.

Naaman had this experience—do you remember the story? As much as he preferred to take a dunk in the Syrian springs, those springs couldn't heal him. God directed him to Palestine to take a swim in foreign waters. There, in the very place he didn't want to be, Naaman found healing.

Does it really matter how light and help come to us? *Where* they come from—now, that's the crucial thing. Where they come from is crucial, but how help gets to us . . . that's not so important. The water is necessary, but the pipe that pumps the water to us is almost inconsequential. If the way God provides help stretches our faith, forcing us to distrust our own ingenuity, if it encourages us toward humility and simplicity and recognizing our need, then God has given a good pipeline. Open up the pool in your heart then, and receive whatever God sends your way, however he sends it.

You might as well surrender to God's aid. If God intends to give help, help is on the way whether we want it or not. As the apostle John says, "The wind blows wherever it pleases." We don't need to know God's secrets. We have a challenge in obeying all that God has already put out in the open. If we spin our wheels trying to decipher the intricate details of what God might be up to, this distracts us from God's obvious presence right in front of our face.

Those who give their energy to high-sounding reasoning appear wise, but they don't have *spiritual* wisdom. Their pseudo-wisdom isn't God-wisdom. In fact, all the wind their wild energy creates blows God's Spirit right out of their lives. The pseudo-wise blow the Spirit out, just as a breeze blows out a candle. If we spend much time with these candle-blowing people, we will notice our heart's flame snuffed out. Our mind will be pulled away from God, its center. Don't interact with these kinds of people. Danger is all they have to offer you.

There are also those who appear spiritually awakened, but this spiritual awakening is only skin deep, a deception. When we encounter someone with a little fire or fresh perspective, we can easily mistake the energy for true spiritual fervor. Here's how to tell if you are running up against a sham: you will notice the person always on the move, frenetically running after some supposed good. What they sprint after will always be external, though, not a quiet work in the soul. Yet they will insist on the chase. Obsessed, they will forever try to figure out how to make this external (supposed) good come to fruition. They forever talk about it. They forever try to figure out every nuance and strip every mystery. In the end, they might capture plenty of facts, but they won't know much about God. They won't know about quietness, a peace, in the soul. They won't know how to listen to God.

These "spiritual" people are all the more dangerous because they appear pious. Their ways are more dangerous because their bluster carries a spiritual label. They live in deception. They hide behind a false persona. If you look deep enough into one of their hearts, you will find a person in constant upheaval, judgmental, chaotic, addicted to activity, unkind, and vulgar. They think solely of their desires (desires that are insatiable). They won't let another person contradict them. To say it straight, I consider them obnoxious spiritual addicts.

To a Religious God-resister

Dear friend,

Let's not play games. You know exactly what God wants from you. Your only question is whether or not you are going to obey. You have given yourself to all kinds of introspection. You've considered every angle, and you've come to the conclusion that your resistance to the pull of grace is due to your pride.

Correct. Now what?

Will you continue allowing pride to determine who you will be? Will you continue allowing your self-willed mind to create these wild realities that have nothing to do with the truth or with who you really are? Are you going to hold onto the vaporous delusions instead of gripping tight to the sturdy mercy of God?

Here's the irony: you take entirely too seriously impulses and feelings that aren't even sinful while you ignore sure-fire evil that could destroy you. You rip yourself apart with guilt for every slight, passing thought. Yet you didn't conjure up the thought. You didn't surrender to fantasy with it. The thought comes and goes, as thoughts do. That's what happens with a human. You are human, you know. So you've done nothing wrong, but still, you lash yourself with condemnation. Out of shame and guilt, you confess as wickedness many things that only deserve a mere shrug of the shoulders.

Remarkably, on the other hand, you seem unconcerned with your continual resistance to the quieter work of God in your life. God isn't working as you suspect he should. God isn't bringing about the results you expect (big, splashy, obvious results). He isn't out in the open. God isn't making you look good, like a spiritual elite. But these demands you make of God are selfish, aren't they? They serve only to make you look admirable and to help you hold a tight rein on your life. Your demands have nothing to do with God and grace.

What do you care if you receive grace the way a beggar receives bread? The gift of God is grace, beautiful and nourishing, even when you are so desperate that all you can do is open your hands and, as a beggar, say "thank you." However, if God gave you grace because your heart was so attractive, so "spiritual" that he couldn't refuse you, then it wouldn't be grace, would it?

You keep thinking you need to be so put-together that God **has** to offer you his goodness. Remind me here: how exactly does this way of thinking combat your pride? What does this kind of self-effort have to do with a relationship with God that is grown by *faith*? This is a very strange way to attempt to die to self: by expecting the self to do miles of work in order to earn God's favor.

While I'm asking questions, can you remind me what you hope to gain by all your spiritual readings and study about the love of God? What are you hoping to accomplish with all the time you are spending in your private devotions? How are you able to read about pure love when it speaks so harshly against the way your soul (with all its effort and self-obsession) is closed off to actually *receiving* God's pure love? Stop reading about love. Receive it. When God offers you mercy and friendship in a way you don't prefer (a way that doesn't contribute to your looking "good" or "spiritual"), then it is only pride and self that cause you to shove grace away.

You love to pray, I know. But how can you pray? Do you know the language God speaks? God speaks words of death to the self, but all you speak of are ways for the self to gain more strength. How can you pray for God's grace when you attach demands that grace can come only if it makes you look good?

Third Conversation

How Do I Hear God?

Few questions have bothered humanity more than this one:

does God speak to us?

Some of us answer no and conclude

there is no God. Some of us answer

yes (or maybe), leading us to

probe further: if God does talk

to us, why don't we hear

the voice more

c l e a r l y ?

These are a few of the questions we are seeking God's voice on: Who am I supposed to marry? What am I supposed to do with my life? Should we have more kids? Any kids? Does God really even care who I marry or what I do with my life? How do I know? Why won't God tell me?

If our sons are afraid or have a question, my wife Miska and I encourage them to talk to God. One night, Wyatt, our four-year-old, followed our advice; but he was irritated because he couldn't hear any voice answering. Apparently God wasn't talking. Miska told him to wait, to be quiet, and to listen with his heart more than with his ears. Wyatt waited impatiently for a few minutes and then lodged a complaint: "God, I still can't hear you. . . ."

Aren't we in that place often? Waiting. Trying to listen. But we just can't hear anything? Thankfully, Wyatt has his mother as a guide. She knows a bit about ways of listening, ways that have less to do with our ears and more to do with our heart. Wyatt needs a guide to help him to learn the language God speaks.

I don't think we are entirely strangers to this language of God. I just think it is a language rarely nurtured in humans. And if this way of speaking and listening lies dormant too long, we forget the unique syntax and the mysterious idiom. Most of us have forgotten how to hear God. In this high-octane world where we demand immediate cause and effect, ask questions and expect instant answers, there is little space for a subtler conversation, one rich in imagination and relationship. There is little space for prayer.

No wonder it is so hard to hear. We have grown accustomed to conversations that are brittle, useful, requiring nothing of us other than an exchange of vowels and consonants and functional signals. Our conversations aim to get the job done.

God's conversation, on the other hand, aims to bring us into friendship with him and to begin the long work of changing us to our core. We have to relearn the art of conversing with God. We need friends, like Fénelon, who have practiced it over many years, to teach us what they know.

WINN COLLIER

To a Confused Listener

Dear friend,

I beg you; don't listen to that small voice, the self-voice. It can get crazy: the self-voice whispering in one ear and the God-voice (love) whispering in the other. The self-voice never stops; it constantly churns. The self-voice is brash, full of energy, and forever trying to force quick, impulsive decisions. This voice seduces us with its intoxicating charms and charisma. In truth, though, the self-voice is short-sighted and hot-headed.

The God-voice is simple, peaceful. It doesn't offer lots of chatter. The God-voice uses only a few words, and God's tone is mild and gentle. The quietness of God's voice poses a dilemma. It is hard to hear the quiet God-tones, those sounds of love, because when we listen to the rambunctious self-voice screaming in our ear, the piercing volume drowns God out.

Each voice that speaks our name has a narrow interest. Each is concerned with only one thing. The self-voice is locked onto (you guessed it) *self.* This voice believes it is absolutely impossible to ever think about yourself too much. The self-voice obsesses to know exactly what everyone's opinion is of us, who likes us and who doesn't, who will feed our ego and who won't. The self-voice sulks unless someone drones on about how fabulous we are, how beautiful, how good.

The other voice speaks in exactly the opposite manner. The God-voice (and remember, I said we could also call this voice **love**) wants self to be forgotten. The God-voice tells us that our self-infatuation is an idol and needs to be ripped down, crushed, and shattered. While the self-voice wants to make us our own god, the God-voice intends to **be** our God. Imagine that. God wants to collect all the energy and love we throw at ourselves.

Here's what we do—silence this useless self-voice. Maybe then we can get some quiet. Maybe then we can actually hear love, hear the God-voice. The God-voice won't force its way in. That's not the way God works. God wants to speak to us, and God waits until we want to listen.

To a Friend Desiring to Know the Future

Dear friend,

Don't get all twisted up about the future. This worry pushes against grace, always at odds with what God does in you and around you. Whenever God hands you something good, something joyful and pleasurable, enjoy what God is giving of himself in the gift. Just eat it up, all of it. Don't hoard it, afraid that God might never be so kind again. Do you remember how God gave the Israelites manna, honey-bread that fell from the sky onto the ground? God told them to gather just enough for each day, to enjoy it, and not to worry about whether or not it would come the next day. You do the same.

There are two unique truths about a sincere faith. First, while many subtle forces attempt to hide God, true faith always sees God—and only God—at work, right in the middle of the action. Second, true faith never delivers the sort of human certainty we constantly look for. True faith won't let us grab hold of safety or latch onto dry formulas. True faith won't let us make an unflinching rule based on God's prior action. What brings us comfort and peace *this* time won't be God's way *next* time. If we drew relief from predictable patterns, we'd trust *that* instead of trusting God. God will do what God will do. He is God, you know. We must surrender, and we must wait and obey and hope in whatever God hands to us.

This kind of day-by-day dependence (just like Israel and the manna) is a paradox. It is both dark and peaceful. It is dark because we truly don't know how the future will play out. We give ourselves to a silent death, death by a slow fire, just like Christian martyrs of earlier centuries. They gave their lives, and so, in our own way, we must too. But this silent flame is hard to perceive. You might not see it. Those who love you might not see it. But God is burning away all you have depended on. God is burning away everything except himself. But don't worry. As I said, this day-by-day dependence, this slow, burning death is not only dark, it is also peaceful. After the burning, God will give you back everything you need. Remember, God brings life out of death.

So, like Israel, eat your bread today and don't worry about tomorrow, because, as Matthew's Gospel says, "Tomorrow will worry about itself. Each day has enough trouble of its own." Let tomorrow worry about tomorrow. God is feeding you today, and this same God is the one for you to depend on again for food tomorrow. This I know: before you (or any of God's children) go without a single morsel that you need, manna will fall out of the sky again, right into the middle of our desert.

To a Friend Wondering What Prayer Is

Dear friend,

Prayer is just another name for loving God. We think that the more words we pile on (and the bigger the better), the more we are praying.

No.

God is your Father, and he knows what you need before you ever ask. Good prayer arises from a place deeper than a barrage of pious words. Genuine prayer emerges from the heart. And the heart is a place of intense passion, a place of desire. To pray, then, is to desire, wanting and hoping for all the good God wants and hopes for us.

If your words are not drenched with desire, then they are not prayer. Say all the words you like. Run through all your lists. Discipline yourself with rigid austerity. Despite all your effort, there isn't a single true prayer among all your religious activity if heart-churning desire isn't part of the mix.

That said, there aren't many of us who truly pray. Few of us crave the genuinely good. We don't like the Cross. We don't like being humbled. We can't stand it when we fail to snag what our greed demands. Basically, whenever God is in charge instead of us, we wince. But all these uncomfortable places are what God calls *good*. Odd, isn't it? If we don't crave this kind of strange good, we aren't praying. But if we do crave it—and if we stick with the craving and go after it—then honest prayer is everywhere.

Many of us are so loaded up with ourselves, trying so hard to be perfect Christians mouthing perfect prayers, that we have never really prayed, not once. Saint Augustine said the same: If you love only a little, then you pray only a little. If you love a lot, then you pray a lot.

Others, however, can't help praying; it's always spilling out. Wherever we discover a heart filled with desire and love for God, prayers are taking shape with every word, every action, every hope.

God takes great delight in seeing our raw desire for him (the desire he put there to begin with) grow in us, pregnant and about to burst. We might not see how virile our desire is, but God does. And it thrills him. It makes God want to pour more mercy and grace on us.

To a Friend Wondering How to Pray

Dear friend,

Whenever we talk about prayer, an obvious question always arises: *how?* We want the particulars—exactly how are we to pray? The answer can be elusive. There is no one way. Each of us has our own way. We need to pay attention to the uniqueness of who we are and how we connect to God. What has worked for us before? If you are disciplined and like structure and regimen, then keep it up. If you find joy in schedules and lists, then have at it. The more boundaries, the better. On the other hand, if you are a free spirit and just the thought of a list makes you cringe, then pray in whatever manner fits you, whatever works.

For you free-birds, make sure you don't scoff at the way others find connection to God. What boxes you in might set another person loose. Also, only the arrogant forget that many wise Christians have followed disciplined ways of prayer for many years. Respect this way of prayer, even if you don't find it helpful. The bottom line is that any method or plan for prayer has only one purpose: to help us pray. If it doesn't help, you can't get rid of it fast enough.

This is the easiest, most natural way I have found to start learning to pray: Pick up a book and pay attention as you are reading. When something in the book grabs you, stop reading. Sit there. Listen to it. Let it feed you. Whenever it seems that you've heard all you're supposed to hear there, then start reading again.

Here's a spiritual rule of thumb: when something connects with us deeply, lighting a little fire in us or giving us joy, then

God is speaking. Whenever something offers a real-world connection to something we are struggling with or some path we are to follow, then God is probably speaking. This isn't hard. Trust what God is saying, and obey it. Don't hesitate. You'll know soon enough if it is God. The Scripture says that when the Spirit is at work, the result is wide-open freedom.

Soon enough, you won't have to second-guess whether or not it is God you hear. You won't always be asking, "Is it God? Is it God?" You'll know (at least more often). It is something you will feel, something your heart will know. The more you listen to God's voice, the more this creative voice will transform the way you see and live in the world. Your heart will become full, joyful, enlivened. As life seeps in, you won't even be desperate to hear God all the time. The pleasure you take from hearing God just once will fuel you for long stretches.

There is a straightforward way to know if you are growing in conversing with God. If your prayers are becoming more simple and if your conversation requires less (fewer words, fewer worries), then you are moving into deeper ways of prayer. Conversation with God is friendship. Like any friendship, when it first starts out, there are a thousand things to talk about as you get to know one another. However, after a while, as the friendship deepens, there are fewer facts to discover about the other. The words are fewer, but the pleasure in being together is as rich as ever. There is little to say, but there is still deep joy. You know a sign of good friendship, don't you?—when you can be silent together and it isn't awkward. You just sit quietly, with nothing to say. And it is good.

To a Friend in Need of Simplicity

Dear friend,

Nothing gives me more satisfaction than to see you living simply, peacefully. Simplicity takes us back home, to the Garden of Eden. There, in our Eden-like life, everything is quiet, simple, and even. There is a little bit of pleasure, but not too much. There is a little bit of pain, but—again—not too much. We aren't consumed by the need to have more, and we are able to be thankful for whatever comes our way, even if it's hard. This quietness in our soul, this freedom from the loudness of fear and the boisterous noise of always watching out for ourselves, gives us a calm contentedness.

Contentment is actually one of the most hedonistic pleasures we can enjoy. Live here. Live in Eden, as God intended all along. Be careful, though. Don't bite the apple. Don't leave simple Eden because you think you need to know more or have more. Like Adam and Eve, you can't handle the knowledge of good and evil. That's only for God.

You are never less alone than when you are sharing life with a single faithful friend. You are never in less danger than when the All-powerful carries you in his arms. Nobody brings us help the way God does. Even when God sends us comfort through another human, the help isn't coming from that person. Left alone, that person, that friend, is dried up and has nothing to give. God is giving himself through that friend. And so, when God is pouring himself into your heart, you don't actually **have** to have human help.

Remember this from the book of Hebrews: "In the past God spoke to our ancestors through the prophets at many times and in various ways, but in these last days he has spoken to us by his Son. . . ." Does it make any sense then, when Jesus is speaking directly to us, to pine away for the feeble voice of the prophets? When God speaks directly to our soul, his voice is powerful and clean. It is all we need. Often it won't be what you expect, though. At times God goes mute in all the ways you are used to hearing him. That is when you can have full confidence that God is in fact speaking. Listen carefully.

Fourth Conversation

What Do I Do When I'm Broken Down?

We are a broken, tired, listless, and lifeless generation.

The clichés are many:

rat race, merry-go-round, burnout.

The damage to our soul is not a

cliché, though. It is

s e r i o u s

b u s i n e s s .

Recently I had a conversation with a friend who has been promoted to management in a fast, high-powered field of business. He is young, with a fresh graduate degree, and has been married only a few years. His spiritual path has taken him on just as quick a pace as his career path. He has seen God do good work in his heart. He has become more the man God has in mind for him to be. He has taken on leadership in his spiritual community, and his impact is very real.

But he is tired. He sat on my couch and asked, "How do I stop?"

His weariness has multiple contributing factors. His childhood story is unfortunately common. The family's public persona was healthy and loving. However, under the veneer, there was emotional disengagement and anger and manipulation. My friend had to learn to fend for himself. As he went through high school and college, his path was scattered with unhealthy relationships and numerous attempts to exert his considerable personality and charisma and talents to make his life work. When he moved into adulthood with all the complexities of marriage and his emerging manhood and his deepening spiritual desires, he has found that his muscle and skill and craftiness were simply not enough for him to manage life. It isn't just that life is hard (though this is true). It's also that he wants more of life than what he is able to scratch out for himself.

He has spent his whole life working and struggling, putting all his mental and physical weight toward wrestling with whatever challenge needed to be overcome or whatever relationship needed to be strengthened. And it isn't enough. It never is.

My wife, Miska, listened to his story. She cares about our friend; he's family. She heard him, truly heard him (and what a rare gift that is). She acknowledged his weariness and offered him true compassion. However, she knew he needed more than compassion. She asked him, in that gentle, direct way she has, "I wonder if you are frantic with all this work and activity because you have tied your worth to the outcome?" The question landed someplace raw and deep. Our friend saw his heart in a way he hadn't before, and he saw the hopeful possibility of living another way.

This is what good spiritual guides will do when we have broken souls. They will listen to us and love us and truly hear us with much compassion. And then they will seek to ask us a question or tell us a truth that will move us toward healing, toward Jesus.

WINN COLLIER

To a Spiritually Lethargic Friend

Dear friend,

Peace. Just sit in it. It's not your job to work up passion and fiery devotion for God. It doesn't depend on you. All you can do, all you are responsible to do, is to choose the one you will obey. Hand your will, your obedience, over to God. Don't hold anything back.

Frankly, it's irrelevant how much intense feeling you have in your spiritual life right now. The more important question to ask is this: *Do I want what God wants?* Humbly confess your faults. Don't hold onto your world. Abandon yourself to God. Choose to love God more than you love yourself. Desire God's name to be made great. Desire God to have God's way—want that more than you want your own life. If you don't feel these things, then just *want* to feel it, hoping you will someday. In the meantime, ask God to give you this kind of love for him. He will. God will love you, and he will pour peace into your heart.

To a Friend Obsessed with His Faults

Dear friend,

Don't be concerned about your defects. Rather than being consumed with yourself, love. Don't stop loving. As Luke's Gospel reminds us, when we have been forgiven much, we love much. Love will overcome your faults.

The problem, however, is that often we want all the warm feelings and immediate perks love brings, but we don't really want love itself. We deceive ourselves because all our hard work trying to love well isn't really for the sake of love. We often use love as yet one more self-absorbed benchmark to measure and demonstrate our (perceived) robust spiritual life. We are trying to make sure we are doing right, that we love *right*.

When we do this, St. Francis de Sales tells us that we are more occupied with the notion of love than with the person of love: Jesus. If all we pursued was Jesus, then he would consume our energy rather than all our effort alone consuming our energy. Whenever we exert our sweat trying to make sure we do the right things (i.e., that we love the right way) in an effort to make Jesus love us in return, we aren't loving Jesus. Rather, we are fixated on ourselves. If we continue to catalog our faults, hoping to muster up our own goodness to overcome these faults, then we are anxious, never at rest. We block God's healing presence. We interrupt the ways God wishes to heal us with his love. However, when we take honest stock of our faults, resting in Jesus' peace and love to overcome them, we witness this powerful force—love—doing exactly that. Love will overwhelm and consume all that we think is so despicable.

Then, so simply, these faults are gone.

Here's the irony: usually, the shame you feel for your faults is actually more of a fault than those things you are so obsessed with. You are completely absorbed with the smaller fault. It's like a person I just spent some time with. After he read about the life of one of the saints, he was so angry at his imperfections that he completely gave up on the idea of living a life devoted to God.

I am able to see how faithful you are to God by how much peace and freedom you have in your soul. When your heart is peaceful, opening up wide to God and the world around you, then you are moving closer to God.

To a Friend Who Needs to Stop Trying So Hard

Dear friend,

Right now, you are in excessive distress. Your despair is running wild, like a summer hurricane. Unfortunately, we are simply going to have to allow this pain to run its course. I know that in this place there is nothing that gives you joy, nothing that sparks any hope. I know you have a frightening, chaotic imagination, and because the craziness in your head seems so real, you are becoming convinced that the most outrageous things your brain tells you must be true. Don't be too unnerved by all this—this is what happens when you face great suffering. Do you realize that this is where you are—in the middle of **great** suffering? However, God is doing something in the middle of all this insanity.

Even though you are perceptive and have a great mind, God will allow the chaos to converge in such a way that none of your natural abilities are any help. On the one hand, you will be blind, unable to see what is plain as day, three feet in front of you. On the other hand, you will be turned so inside out that you will think you see clearly things that don't exist at all. If you can just stay with this and allow God to finish what he is up to, God will have what he wants— your heart will be God's. While you are waiting, though, be very careful not to make a serious mistake. Don't come to conclusions about anything while swamped in the middle of such distress. This isn't the time for deciding or for doing. God isn't asking you to **do** anything. Just wait. Right now, do nothing.

Later, after things have calmed down and you are more at rest, you can quietly and peacefully consider your circumstances and evaluate the truth of your situation. Then, when you aren't so ruffled, you can get a simple sense of what might be best for you. Again, it will be simple stuff. Gradually go back to simple living, simple listening, simple praying, simple humility. Don't rush. Give yourself time. Have ears wide open to God, and have ears closed shut to self. After that, just do whatever is in your heart, whatever you want to do, whatever makes you come alive. Don't worry about doing the wrong thing. If you are living this way (simply listening to God and your own heart), you aren't going to do the wrong thing.

However, you aren't in this simple, quiet place right now. Your mind isn't clear, and you can't think clearly when you are in the middle of agony and distress. Right now, you are facing a violent temptation to think too much about yourself—and too little about God. Right now, in this place, you are almost assured of doing the wrong thing. You can ask any spiritual advisor experienced in the ways of God and in the ways of the human soul. They will tell you to do nothing. Don't make any decisions about what you are to do or what any of this means until you have came back to a place of peace and calm. The quickest and most certain way to deceive yourself is to trust yourself when you are in the middle of suffering. You can't think straight here. Your mind and your spirit are agitated and disheveled, not at rest. So, again, do nothing.

I know what you are thinking. You feel like I am holding you back from obeying God. You are wildly restless. You believe you must make a decision this very moment, right now. You can't wait. As soon as you sense any supposed spiritual impulse, your compulsive behavior kicks in. So, with your spiritual neurosis, you think I am standing in the way of your obeying God.

Nothing could be further from the truth. The last thing I want is to get in the way of your spiritual growth. The one thing I want for you is to guide you so that God is able to do everything in you he desires to do. I will be brutally honest with you. One thing I know for sure—you will never see God finish this work in you if you listen to the temptation to do something right now. I know you are in pain, and I know you have a compulsion to make it go away. I know that your soul is agitated and restless and on the verge of despair. However, ask yourself this—do you really want to relieve the pain and pressure if relief is not what God wants for you right now? God forbid!

Wait, then. Wait until you can listen and are in a place to receive spiritual guidance. If you really want to enjoy all the good that comes with spiritual illumination, then be prepared for every way this illumination might come—even if the light comes first under the guise of darkness.

To a Friend Who Must Give Herself Kindness

Dear friend,

We all have to shoulder our crosses, and self is the most difficult cross of all.

If you would like a signal that indicates your addiction to self is broken, I will give you one. When you are able to be as patient and kind to yourself as you are to others, giving yourself as much space as you would someone else, self-absorption is gone. But not until then.

If we die to ourselves a little bit every day of our lives, we won't have much dying to do at the end. The death we dread in the far future won't actually be very frightening when it arrives because we won't be sucked in by its exaggerated terrors. We will have already learned the practice of wiggling free from the fear of losing ourselves.

Give yourself plenty of space. Allow yourself to be what you are, where you are. You will need help, though. Humbly allow your friends to help you and love you by caring for you, even (particularly) when your weakness makes you most self-conscious and most vulnerable. These little daily deaths will take away the sting of your final death.

To a Friend Who Must Make a Decision

Dear friend,

The truth is that I am quite fascinated at how much good is imbedded in suffering. Isn't it strange—we are actually destitute *without* the cross. I feel the crushing force. I can barely hold up. I think I will buckle under the strain. I won't lie—it's agony. In these torture moments, all my high-sounding conviction of how valuable and helpful these stretching experiences will ultimately be evaporates.

But when the suffering has passed, I look back at the experience; and I appreciate the experience. I respect what God has done with my discomfort. I am even ashamed that I cursed the pain while things were painful. My ignorant, short-sighted response to the struggle teaches me a deep, wise lesson.

Concerning your friend, the one who is sick, I don't know all her circumstances. However, whatever sickness she faces, she is blessed, since she is able to rest quietly as God's hand presses in on her. If she dies, she dies leaning into Jesus. And if she lives, she then lives leaning into Jesus. *Either the cross or death,* says St. Teresa. Apparently, there is a death either way.

There is no season or place where we do not need the cross— except of course when God's kingdom has its final, complete rule. Whenever we take on the cross in love, God's kingdom has begun then and there. We must choose whether or not we will endure the cross and stick with our suffering. You have need of the cross, and so do I. The faithful Giver who gives every good gift is the one who hands out crosses to each of us. God does it with his own hand, and I thank him even for the suffering.

To a Weak Christian

My dear daughter,

You need to do only one thing. Endure the sufferings you experience in your body and in your mind. Don't give up. And don't worry about doing anything other than bearing your pain with hope and grace. This is plenty of spiritual work for you now.

Do you remember the strange thing Scripture says? Strength actually finds its full capacity when it is surrounded by weakness. *When I am weak,* says St. Paul, **then I am strong.** We are desperate for God's strength, but we can't receive it unless we surrender the silly ways we clutch onto our own strength. This is how it works: we let our (supposed) strength drain out, and then God's strength fills up the space. The bizarre reality is that your weakness will actually be the very thing that allows you to find the genuine strength you need. Your responsibility is not to create your own vigor but rather to humbly accept that you are weak and God is strong.

I am asking you to fully abandon yourself to God. I know that we tend to think that humility and weakness somehow interfere with this kind of absolute abandonment to God. We think of abandonment as a heroic act of epic love that makes stunning, courageous, grand sacrifices for God. It's actually a lot simpler than that. True abandonment just gives itself over, just rests in God's care and love, like a baby in its mother's arms. Here's the tricky thing: true abandonment has to abandon even its abandonment. We have to give up our self-inflated sense of what a big sacrifice we are making. We need to give up on ourselves without even thinking much of it. If we spend time pondering how much we are abandoning for God, everything is short-circuited. Nothing will be more help to you in all this than completely, fully, giving up—even giving up how hard you are trying to give up.

True abandonment is not doing large spiritual acts that you can be proud of, thinking you've done something great. True abandonment simply holds up under the humbling process, leaving it alone and letting God do what God will do.

Abandonment is peaceful. If we are anxious about whatever it is we have abandoned, then we can't really call it **abandonment**, can we? However, if we have truly given ourselves over and surrendered fully, not even concerned with the angst of being abandoned, then we have peace, real peace. If we don't have peace, it shows that we haven't really abandoned ourselves yet—we are still holding on.

Fifth Conversation

How Do I Cultivate A Quiet Soul?

Entering the Apple Store is risky business for me.

It's amazing how many things there are

that I didn't know I needed until I enter the

G a r d e n   o f   T e m p t a t i o n

(the logo is a freshly bitten apple, after all).

The technological possibilities are infinite.

It's as if I can hold the world in my

p o c k e t .

In this culture, we are awash in gadgets and bandwidth and apps of every sort. With virtually no effort, we can connect (if we can be generous enough to call it that) with the singles' scene in our own ZIP code or with an old friend nine time zones away. The information available boggles the mind. The speed and efficiency of modern life has fueled an economic boom. There are perks, for sure, to living in the digital age. But it hasn't helped us with a uniquely spiritual dilemma: our acute need to nurture a quiet, restful soul.

The Mac revolution did not create this problem for us. Spiritual wanderers of every generation have struggled to discover how to still the external noise so they can pay attention to their souls. One may have wrestled with quieting the Roman Empire's false values. Another may have felt the constant, heavy noise of the Industrial Age: produce, produce, produce! Another may now find herself in rhythm with a steady strain of noises demanding time, attention, and loyalty. We are addicted to activity. There is something in the fallen human heart that resists sitting—simply sitting—in the still place, the slow place, where nothing is at work . . . nothing other than God.

We might be tempted to think that the easy answer is to give ourselves to spiritual activity, and the problem is solved. Fénelon's guidance tells us the answer is often just the contrary. He suggests that filling up on so-called spiritual exercises is one of the worst culprits in filling our soul full of noise. False spirituality often impulsively pushes us to do more, to speak more, to serve more, to quit more bad habits. We are to become more introspective, more ascetic, more determined. More. More. More. And the noise is so, so loud.

Do you want to move into quiet? Do you desire to be at odds with virtually every cultural presence around you? I do, but I need someone to guide me there. I know my addiction to activity and noise and chaos, and I want to change. How do I do it? How do I begin the long work of cultivating a quiet soul?

WINN COLLIER

To a Spiritually Overactive Friend

My dear young friend, live in peace.

You are a woman called to live free from the worry of trying to figure out what is going to happen with you. You can't know the answer. You can't control what will happen. Maybe **nothing** will happen with you. Even what you have now—the present—really isn't yours. Even **the now** is God's. You must live in the present in ways God has mapped out, not in ways you have drawn up for yourself.

Keep living your life, serving God as you enjoy doing. I know that what you are doing now comes easily for you, so keep it up. Don't get distracted. Tone down your feverish pace and your uber-activity—nothing good ever comes of that. Stay connected to the present moment. Stick with it. If you do, you will have all the grace you need. Best of all, you will **receive** grace, and you won't have to work to get it.

We might think that all we need to worry about is being unchained from the values of our culture. Actually, there is something else. We also need to learn humility. When we eschew our culture's values, we are saying no to mostly external things, all the dark stuff that is pushed on us from the outside. However, when we are humble, we are saying no to ourselves, all the dark stuff lurking in our own hearts. Any pride that we detect needs to be abandoned, every little bit.

We need to be particularly on the lookout for the pride that likes to attach itself to spiritual activity. When we think we are growing wise in God's ways (getting lots of spiritual knowledge) and when we think we are becoming quite virtuous (doing or saying the right things), watch out! This is dangerous stuff.

In fact, it is more dangerous than a lot of the more external concerns, the obvious sins the culture wants to press on you. Spiritual pride is harder to detect. It seems milder and often works under the guise of spiritual maturity.

So we need to be humble top to bottom. We should never think that we are the cause of our spiritual growth. We aren't the ones building virtue into our lives. We aren't the ones giving ourselves courage to live boldly in our world. Let me speak plainly: you trust in yourself too much. You think it is your courage moving you forward. You think it is your spiritual austerity that is keeping you from sin. You think it is your own virtue and strong conviction that is building your Christian character.

None of this is true.

A baby doesn't have anything it can really call its own. It isn't enamored of the small or the great—a diamond and an apple are all the same to her. Then why not be like a spiritual baby? Don't hold onto all the things you suppose are yours. Forget yourself. Give away the silly notions that you are some super-spiritual person or that you have all the right answers or that you can do some great work for God. Unplug from all that pressure, and let everyone else and everything else take the front. You move quietly to the back.

Keep your prayers simple; make them heart-prayers. Pray what you feel, what you love, not what you think, not just what you have reasoned out. You will learn spiritual truths, but you won't learn the way (or the *what*) you imagined. All your well-crafted plans will probably be spoiled. You will give lots of space to quiet and soul-deep thinking and journeying. You will need to come into a deep silence, with your entire self—body, mind, and spirit—silent, quiet, and restful before God.

You will need to say no to the internal, self-inflated voices. Fall in love with humility and with being obscure, unnoticed. Be okay with being feeble and broken. Be okay with the death that will come to your self-constructed spirituality. It doesn't seem right, but as you begin to come to terms with all the questions you *don't* have the answers for, truth will find its way to you. On your own, your so-called knowledge could never make that happen.

To a Friend Who Cannot Stop

Dear friend,

There are many good qualities that might make us attractive to others while helping us get a lot done: awakened creativity, passionate emotions, a finely tuned mind, and the ability to communicate with flair. These are nice traits, but they don't get much of the real stuff done, the God-stuff. If we really want to see spiritual work accomplished, we need to give all of it up, abandoning all of our "good stuff" to God. Rather than constantly trying to manufacture our own manic light, we just wait for whatever light God gives—and then follow that. Next, we learn to be content with whatever God makes happen, big or small. This abandonment, this death to all our self-stuff, is the only way to live a full and joyful life. Unfortunately, not many live this good life.

We think we need to say a lot. We don't. Just a single word, spoken out of rest—out of waiting for and following after God—will do more than all our hyperactivity, more than all the sweat we exert putting our shoulder into the so-called "spiritual" work. Even then, with our one single word of hope or faith or love, we aren't really the ones doing the talking anyway. The Spirit of God is speaking. And when the Spirit speaks, there is energy we could never muster. There is authority, strength. The Spirit illuminates what is dark, motivates us to move into action, and teaches us all the truth we need. This is when a paradox is evident. We have done all the work that needs to be done, and we have barely uttered a word, barely lifted a finger.

There is another way this can play out, though. If, rather than resting, we follow our addiction to frantic activity, we talk forever, using lots and lots of words. We talk a lot about *nuance*, and we talk in circles about a thing, using words that sound wise and intelligent but never really go anywhere. We talk so much because we are afraid. We are afraid that we won't get it right, that we won't say something we should have said or that we won't do something we were supposed to do. What happens next is inevitable. We get angry. We get irritable and restless. We grow exhausted and are entirely un-centered. Then, truly *nothing* gets done. *We're* done; we're empty.

I know you—you have the kind of personality that struggles with obsessive behavior. You especially need to hear me on this. This is important for your whole person, for the health of your body as well as for the health of your soul. It's a holistic healing you need—both your medical doctor and your spiritual guide need to know how compulsive and driven you are. Your soul as well as your body will be included on your path of healing.

Learn to let your neurotic fixations go. Learn to let humans be just that—*human*. Since we are human, that means we are broken, selfish, fickle, unjust, untruthful, and arrogant. Learn to let the world be what it is—fallen. The world isn't as it was intended to be; accept that. Otherwise, you really are going to wear yourself out. Learn to give people space. Give them room to be who they are, having their own bents and struggles and ways of living. Make peace with this: you can't change people. Let them be and live with them, exactly where they are.

Don't be surprised when you see people acting in ways that make no sense or when you see people perpetrating injustice. Rest. Give way to peace. Trust in God. It's God's world, and God sees all that is happening far more clearly than you do (and, apparently, he doesn't see the need to rush in right now and change everything). Be okay with the simpler way. Be okay with a more subversive path. Quietly, restfully, just do whatever you think you should. Ignore the rest.

To a Friend with a Runaway Mind

Dear friend,

Plant and water peace. Ignore your runaway imagination—its incessant noise and revved-up energy does damage to your physical health and makes your soul dry as bones. With activity, you cannibalize yourself, and it is to no good end. Your fidgety ways destroy any possibility of peace or soul rest. Do you think God is able to speak in those hushed and gentle rhythms that melt the soul when you live in the hurricane your frenzy has stirred up in your mind? Be quiet, and God will soon be heard.

Actually, you should be concerned about one thing (but only one): obedience.

You say you want comfort; but you are blind to the fact that you have been led to the very source of the fresh-water spring—and you refuse to drink. Peace and comfort can be discovered only in simple obedience.

Be faithful to obey and pay no attention to the craziness in your mind, to all the guilt and confusion. As you do, you will soon sense the rivers of living water flowing just as God has promised. You will be given as much as your faith is able to receive. Much, if you can believe God wants to give you much. Nothing, however, if you believe in nothing and continue to listen to the dark void your imagination has conjured up.

You trivialize authentic love when you assume that the small things that hold you hostage have also kidnapped love. This isn't true. Love is wild and free; it goes straight to God with abandon and simplicity. Satan masquerades as an angel of light. He disguises himself beautifully, under the garb of things that seem spiritual. He will use a false, overwrought love or a guilt-wracked mind against you. However, you have already experienced the trouble and danger Satan will lead you into with these intense assaults and pressures and guilt. This is serious—you absolutely must have a courageous obedience and push back Satan's very first advances. You must cut him down when he first raises his head or first slings his lies.

If you will be frank and raw with your desires, I think you will please God more than if you undertake some great spiritual feat. Telling God plainly what you want—and letting yourself want it—is better than being martyred a hundred times. Gather up all your worry and all your dread and channel that energy toward this raw desire God longs to see. If we truly love, how could we hesitate when asked to give our God pleasure? We hand God pleasure when we express our truest desires to him.

To an Emotional Wreck

Dear friend,

I am praying for you, asking God to make this new year spill over with grace and blessing for you. You say you aren't enjoying solitude and reflection like you used to, when everything was fresh and new. I'm not surprised. As you remember, when you began this spiritual exercise, you were eager for relief, and you got it. You felt delivered from your long, painful turmoil.

Unfortunately, every new experience eventually wears off. It can be a jolt when persons who are energetic and active, always on the move (like you), find themselves thrust into solitude and stillness. Before long, they are languishing, feeling despair and not knowing what to do with themselves. For years now, the demands of your life have required that you be constantly distracted by all kinds of external stimuli. In fact, your old life habits concerned me. I wondered how you would respond to the new life God invites you to, removed entirely from that frantic way of living. This is quite a contrast, enough to disorient anyone.

Of course, at the beginning when you were excited about a fresh start and the newness of it all, you thought it was easy, nothing to it. It looked like clear sailing to you. You couldn't see how this new, quiet season could ever cause hardship. You see how hard it is *now*, don't you? You're in good company. You remind me of the disciple Peter, who had a brash streak in him, making bold, self-certain claims. He had good intentions, but a lot of times, they were misdirected. When we're feeling pleasure and joy, we think we're invincible. Nothing can stop us. But then, when we're feeling temptation and despair, we think we're useless. Everything is hopeless. Both feelings—invincible and useless—are wrong.

Don't be disturbed by the many distractions you will experience. Don't be surprised by how hard it will be to give yourself quietly and intently to God. Even when you **were** excited about your simple life with God and even when your devotion to God came easily—even then—you possessed the very things that cause you trouble now. They were just crouching in the corner.

Your personality and your habits conspire together, pushing you toward restlessness. Before, you didn't come to solitude naturally. You came only because you were so exhausted that anything felt better than keeping up the insane pace. The truth is that you didn't have a choice—you were too tired to do anything but stop. However, if you will stay committed to allowing God's grace the freedom to work in you, you will grow into being able to actually *live* in this restful way. I know you're frustrated that you've had only a taste of the peaceful life, but trust me, you will learn to drink it in deeply. Be patient. It will take time.

Don't be shocked when you feel edgy, impatient, proud, or rebellious. You have to be allowed to own up to the truth that, left to yourself, this is who you are. You aren't nearly as good as you like to think you are. Saint Augustine says that we have to bear the weight of the constant confusion our sins hurl at us. We must actually feel, deeply feel, how weak we are. We have to see how wretched we are. We have to give up on the strong lie that somehow, if we apply more muscle or figure out a few more answers, we can fix ourselves. We have to give up the thought that we have any hope at all in ourselves. We have to come to the place where we are empty, realizing that if God doesn't rescue us, we're doomed. We have to stop pandering to our egos. We must be honest about our desperate situation. And then, with all this brutal honesty, we must surrender ourselves to whatever means God wants to use to do his rescue work.

God pulls at us from every angle. We have to be shown the truth about the vileness in us, even while we're forced to wait for God to take the vileness away. While waiting, we must bend our heart and let God's heavy hand move where it will, when it will. Whenever you sense the least bit of resistance to what God wants to do, give way. Be silent as much as you can. Don't try to determine what you think God is doing. Don't make any decision right now about what you're supposed to be doing. Don't give too much thought to smaller things, about what you like or don't like in this process. Just be still and peaceful. Whenever you start feeling restless or start feeling compelled to do something, stop. Don't be too eager to get anything, even something good. Right now, you need to be still.

Sixth Conversation

How Can I Live in Community?

One of the beauties—
as well as the
prickly points—
of Christian faith is that it is never
intended to be lived in theory. Faith is fleshed out
among particular people, in particular places.
Some of the most important elements of our
spiritual pilgrimage will be names—names of
friends we've had and places we've lived. There
will be people we couldn't get enough of and
people who hung around way too much.
There will be places that felt like home,
places that felt like hell, and places that
had bits of b o t h .

To live well, we must embrace this particularity. If we don't, we will miss the very best of what it means to be alive. We will miss living with an engaged, open heart. As Terry Tempest Williams said, "If I choose not to become attached to nouns—a person, place, or thing—then . . . my heart cannot be broken because I never risked giving it away."[3]

This isn't easy. The pain is in the particulars. We can believe in the idea of squashing our selfishness in order to love another. We can believe in the notion of giving ourselves to a place that isn't exactly the place we would choose. However, the actual doing of it, the loving and the giving—that often hurts. It hurts because we can't control the process. We can't choose all the people God will send into our life, and we can't choose to turn it all off when it gets too messy.

And it most certainly will be messy. Honest relationships, honest life—these are the ingredients for chaos. As we live in community, we will find many paradoxes. While we will have rich friendships, we will also be awakened to profound loneliness. We will discover more of what it means to love, but we will also experience more about being irritated, disappointed, and put-off. Eugene Peterson says that living in community is learning to live with people you don't like. That seems about right.

Since it is so hard and so vital, this stuff of relationship and community, it is obvious that we need help to learn the way. Every form of Christian community needs a guide to walk it through the years of struggle and living and loving. Every marriage needs to learn from another marriage that's farther along. Every friendship needs to hear from other friendships that have already experienced what they now face. It gets even more basic. Every man needs to know how to engage other men and women. Every woman needs to know how to live in relationship with other women and men. How do we live connected in this disconnected world?

WINN COLLIER

To a Lonely Friend

Dear friend,

We must learn contentment. What God gives, we receive, gratefully. We like to believe that we can choose what God gives to us. We can't. If we got to choose, we would pick only the things we want, not the things God wants. What we really need is this: for God's desires to become our desires, without restrictions, without qualifications. If God wants something, we want it just as much.

Do you remember the prayer we pray: *God, let your will be done here on earth in the same way it is already being done in heaven?* That's what we need—God's will done here, in us. And the good, the beauty, of what we gain when God does what he wants in us, well, it's immense. It's far more valuable than anything you would ever get on your own.

There simply is no community like the community we find when God is what brings us together. Our conversation really flows when what we want and what we are giving our minds to is God. Is it deep soul-friends that you so badly want? Learn to look for friends by looking deeply into God. God is the place that all real friendship, the kind that is sturdy and lasts, flows from. Do you want deep, meaningful conversation with a friend? Go into God. Sink in deep. We want true words, and God is the Living Word. We long for rich life, and God is Life. God has given himself to us, implanted himself deep in us. If we learn to speak and live the truth, we will discover him there.

With God, you will find all you have wanted. It will be even better than that—you will find everything you have never been able to find in any other friend. You have looked for so much from your friends. Much of what you've searched for you have never found. But you will find it in God.

To a Wounded Soul

My dear friend,

Like a good friend should, I feel sorrow for how hard your life is right now. However, the hard truth is that there isn't much I can do to fix it. I can pray to God for you and ask him to comfort you—and I will.

What you need most is for God's Spirit to hold you up and to keep you in one piece. You need the Spirit to push back against your natural tendency, which is to kick into high gear, trying to be chirpy and making everything seem spiffy. You also tend to expend vast amounts of energy trying to alter your situation. I know you, and that's what you often do when your life isn't working. In your letter, you asked what I thought about the situation of your childhood.

I think you need to lay it before God alone. Don't take this into your own hands. Don't try to fix it. Just beg for God to give his mercy to the one who has injured you.

All along, I had thought I sensed that this was a raw place for you—and God always plunges into our rawest places. If you needed to kill something, you wouldn't take a knife and trim its hair. You wouldn't try to kill something by tickling it, would you? No, you would plunge the knife deep, into the organs, right at the places that have to do with death and life. And here it is: God wants us to die to our selves. To do this, God always plunges into the raw places, where we are tender, the places that have to do with death and life. This is how God gives away his cross.

Allow God to humble you. Be quiet. Surrender to peace, knowing that this kind of humility from God is truly good for your soul. There is a real temptation to talk a lot during this process. We can think of a thousand reasons to talk about what God is doing and to talk about how we are being humbled. Don't talk; be humbled silently. If your "humility" is the kind that still loves to talk, watch out. We are in love with ourselves, and we love to hear ourselves talk.

Don't get too bent out of shape by what others say about you. Let people wag their tongues while you worry about obeying God. Besides, you would never be able to meet everyone else's expectations. You couldn't do it, and it isn't worth all the grief to try. For every slander spoken against you, replace it with a moment of silence, of peace, of conversation with God.

We must love others, but we must not demand friendship in return. Friends abandon us and then come back; friends come and go. Take your hands off the relationship and let them do what they will do. Don't try to grasp after them—that's like trying to catch a feather in a windstorm. Learn to see your friends as ones who bring God to you. That way, they aren't really the point; God is. If our friends cause us grief, God is actually giving us grief through them. If our friends bring us pleasure, God is using them to deliver pleasure. God knows what we need, that's for sure.

To a Friend Living with Difficult People

Dear friend,

It has been a long time since I have reminded you of how committed I am to you. I want to live in Jesus-community with you. I know I haven't said it in a while, but the friendship I feel toward you is stronger than ever.

With all my heart, I really do wish that you were able to experience in your home the peace and comfort that you so enjoyed when you first formed this community. It takes work to enjoy even the easiest people. Here are two necessities for living in community and friendship: abandon your many high demands and patiently tolerate the other's annoying behavior. Expect less; put up with more. You heard me say this would require work, right? True community is not for the faint of heart.

The truth is that all of us, even those who seem nearly flawless, have scads of imperfections. If we are around these supposed angelic people long enough, we will see their eccentricities and their blemishes. This shouldn't surprise us—we have a good number of faults ourselves. You have your work cut out for you. You are dealing with two flawed people (you and the other person), and no matter how good your relationship, it will eventually be difficult for both of you to endure the other. This is why we must pick up the slack for the other person in the very place where that one struggles the most (the places where the person is the most annoying). We move toward the other's defects, not away. When we do this, we obey God, walking the Jesus Way. We do what the letter to the Galatians encourages us to do: allow love to balance out each other's shortcomings.

You aren't passive here. You can actually take some specific actions to encourage peace and harmony in your relationship. Be quiet . . . a lot. Regularly corral your mind. Pray. Surrender your addiction to having your way. Renounce your haughty criticisms. Commit to stopping your self-righteous thoughts that rise out of a selfish, harsh demand to get what you want. You have no idea how much of your conflict these simple acts will resolve. If we stop listening to ourselves and to others' gossip, we will be much happier.

Be content with leading a simple life, however that fits for you. Be obedient. Bear your daily cross—you need it. It is a gift given by the pure mercy of God. The essential idea is to despise self from the heart, and to be willing to be despised, if God allows it. Feed upon God alone. Saint Augustine says that his mother lived on prayer. You do the same, and die to everything else. We can live toward God only as we allow our self to continually die.

To a Judgmental Friend

Dear friend,

Your heart needs to grow. The way you respond to others' weaknesses reveals that you have a small heart. I know you can't stop the immediate, subconscious opinions or biases that take shape in your head, wondering what your friends are up to or what angle your friends are playing. What's worse, I know you can't put the brakes on the negative effect others' failings have on you.

But you can do this: put up with your friends' obvious defects. Then, with all the other defects you imagine they might have, don't judge. Don't allow their weaknesses to cast a gray pall over the warmth and friendship you know you do feel for them. Don't let another's imperfections rob you of the beauty of friendship.

The ironic truth is that the person most matured by grace is the same person least annoyed by those of us who are grade-A messes. The large-hearted person accepts people where they are. We shouldn't be surprised when we see gaping defects in good people, and we shouldn't try to fix them or keep using our long finger to point out their faults. Instead, keep quiet. Just let people be and let God dive into their clutter. Our interference will just muddle up the transformation God has in mind. The truth is that, even in the most mature person, God often chooses to leave some weaknesses that seem entirely out of character. Even though God has cleaned much out of this person's soul, God likes to leave reminders of our humanity and our need. Remember, all of this—then and now—is God's work. It isn't ours.

Each of us must do the hard work of participating in the ways God is cleaning us up. And part of **your** hard work is putting up with other people's faults. You know how hard and painful it is when God cleans you up; so, why don't you expend your energy trying to help others' experience be less hard and less painful? Rather than condemning them, comfort them. I know the way you struggle with this: your reaction when you see a friend's fault isn't usually to go and correct the friend, but rather you withdraw, and your heart grows smaller.

Having said all this, don't now hold back when you see my faults. If you think you see a fault in me—and if you are wrong—you really haven't done any harm. Don't worry about it. If your words wound me, then my sensitive reaction proves only that you have discovered some raw place that needs to be revealed. On the other hand, if your words don't wound me, you will have been kind to me, allowing me to exercise humility and to submit to another's correction.

Since I am looked to as a spiritual leader, I have a greater responsibility to live humbly. God demands a more absolute death from me, death in everything. I need this kind of simplicity, and I need it from you. It won't strain our friendship. I believe it will make our friendship all the stronger.

Seventh Conversation

What Do I Do When Life Is Dark and Bleak?

I have two sons,
  Wyatt and Seth.
They are four and three,
  and they are fascinated
    with dragons.
With their play swords and their fierce yells slashing

the air, they charge between the upstairs rooms,

vanquishing these

f i r e - b r e a t h i n g

b e a s t s

from the second story

of our house.

However, rambunctious play gives way to other thoughts that somehow land in the mind of a child. The dragon becomes more than a clawed creature testing their steel; the dragon becomes a metaphor. The dragon is anything dark or scary, every fearful question and every perilous path, all that this cruel world will hurl at a young life. Recently, Wyatt had a sober question to ask me. "If a bad dragon comes," he asked, "will you help me kill the dragon?"

What words for a father to hear! My chest swells, and my blood pumps hard. If such a beast assaults my son, my boy, I will grab its mangy throat and squeeze every last breath from its sulfurous lungs. I am moved because, as a father, I am made for such moments. But I am also moved because I know the question well. The question hits close to home. Each of us, in our own way, wonders the same: When the dragons come, who will help us?

As we grow into who we are becoming, intensity and struggle ensue. Questions grow heavier. At times, hope comes slower. Our inadequacies loom more vivid. In some seasons, it seems dragons are everywhere, waiting to pounce and devour us. We become fixated. Our struggle is not with our sense that we are in the dark. Our struggle is that we feel we are alone.

Most of us are able to make peace with the truth that life is sometimes hard, that we have to muck through places we would rather avoid. Hard and dark. We can deal with that. Fear and despair will not consume us . . . as long as we have a guide. We need a guide who will show us there is nothing to fear, one who will be angry for us, angry against all the terrors in our world. We need a wiser friend who has seen the dark places we are entering and who will walk with us, a bit ahead of us, pointing out the danger spots and telling us with each step that God is always with us.   WINN COLLIER

To a Grieving Heart

My dear sister,

I can't tell you how deeply sorry I am for all the trouble you are facing. However, I don't feel only grief. I also have a strong desire to offer you this comfort: God loves you. Do you know that even this bleakness is a sign of God's love? God cares for you enough to trust you with the cross of Jesus Christ. We may think we have spiritual insight or some vibrant spiritual emotion, but if either wisdom or sentiment does not bring us to the steady experience of dying to ourselves, it is a delusion.

Dying to self: this is the true spiritual path. This is no sunny primrose path, though. May I say the obvious? Death involves suffering. When God blesses us (yes, I said *bless*) with death, it cuts to our core. God knows where the knife needs to land.

This is how God cuts: God slices away at the very things we hold with the tightest grip. It isn't hard for God to find these spots. Whenever God cuts and we wince in pain, our wincing indicates he has sliced into a tender place. This sore spot is hiding something, protecting bits of our self-life. However, we need God-life.

God is a good Father, and he doesn't waste time hacking away at those parts of us that have already died to God. The hard truth is that God isn't most concerned with how to keep us alive. God is most concerned with how to help us die. Die to ourselves. Die to our delusions. Die so we can really live.

Dying hurts, though. God must cut into places full of life (self-life, that is), and there's no way around it—that hurts.

Expect it. God will get tenacious, relentless. God will bore into those gross and evil desires, the same desires you thought were long gone. God might take away the freedom you feel in your soul. God might strip away the person who has brought you comfort or the experience that has provided meaning in your spiritual life. God knows how and where to probe and cut.

Are you going to push back at God in the cutting? No! Don't do that. Be patient. Lean into it. Let God do what he will do. He won't cut more than you allow. You must open yourself up to God. If you resist God in this, your opposition communicates loud and clear: you want to cling to your self-life; you don't want God-life. Lie still under God's knife. Trust God to do good with you.

What are you afraid of? Where is your faith? Do you fear that God isn't big enough, strong enough, to give you whatever you need? Do you fear God might take away a spiritual friendship you share with other people? Do you really think that another person can provide you something that God *cannot* give? The only reason God takes away such relationships is to clear out space for himself in your life. God desires to roll up his sleeves and get busy in your heart. God wants to use the painful experience to clean out the rubbish in your soul.

This is what I see: I see God closing off everything to you, everything but himself. I see God determined to transform you. I see God cutting off every human resource that might distract you from the fresh life he intends to create in you. God is a jealous God. No one else will be able to take credit for your rescue. Only God.

So give yourself over to God's plans. Let God steer you where he will, even if it is headlong into pain and chaos. Avoid sprinting to others for aid if God tells you not to. The reality is that a friend can be helpful only if God has given that person something to pass along to you. Besides, why be discouraged that you can't sip from your usual cup when God is leading you to the gushing stream, the very source of water, of life?

To a Friend Cornered by God

Dear son,

Of course, yes, I am honored that you wish to call me your spiritual father. This brings me joy. I **am** your father. Believe it. Truly receive that I feel this way about you. The larger your heart grows, the easier it will be for you to trust this. Unfortunately, right now, your self-love is closing your heart off from the truth. Whenever we are closed off, holed up in a dark cave with nothing but ourselves, we find ourselves in a small, small place. When we come out of the dark cavern, though, when we step into the bright, warm sunshine, we see how massive God is, how vast God's world is. Then we feel freedom. We see we are God's child, loved and accepted, and then, our heart begins to grow large.

I am actually ecstatic to hear that God has shrunk you to this place where you feel weak and puny. There is no other way your self-love will listen to the truth of God's love, no other way your self-love can be hurled from your heart. Self-absorption is ingenious. It is relentless and clever, always finding little corners of your soul to hide in. Self-love cleverly latches onto some of your natural tenacity, your ability to hold up under pressure. It masquerades as something good. Hidden as it is among admirable qualities, you can't see your self-absorption. It becomes nearly impossible to rip away.

Here's an example: you have a tendency to sacrifice for others, putting what others need before your own needs. That's honorable; but even an honorable act can be a subtle poison, feeding your sense of self, the notion that you are coming to someone's rescue or you are saving the day. It's all about you. So, even in your so-called generosity or nobility, self-love hides.

But God won't let self-love hide. God won't let self-addiction lurk in the shadows, quiet and unseen. God has a way of making the self yelp so we know exactly where to find it. God forces self's hand, provoking the self to uncover its excessive jealousy. This way, God makes our false self slither out of the dark and into broad daylight. The process is intensely painful, I know. The entire operation hurts, but this redemptive pain will do the job. The affliction will reveal what needs to be exposed. As long as any little bit of self-love stays smuggled away, we will fear everything that accompanies the process of our selfishness being uncovered. However, God is not afraid. As long as we have the least bit of self-regard lurking in the shadows of our heart, God goes after it. With mercy, God strikes, forcing self-love out into the open.

After self-love has been pushed into the bright, painful daylight where it cowers, naked and chagrined, this is where the surprise comes. That shameful place actually offers us part of our cure. Self-love, stripped of illusion and yanked from its underground cubbyhole, sees itself truly: small, deformed, puny. At that moment, our prefabricated image crashes. Despair descends. God shows us, right then and there, our idol: self. You see it. You can't look away. You can't escape. You are no longer in control of yourself. The lie—and the truth—are in the open. You can't hide your hideousness from yourself, and you can't hide your hideousness from anyone else.

This seems like terrifying punishment, when self-love's ugliness goes unmasked. We see the unvarnished truth. All our supposed "sacrifice" for others, all our supposed "spirituality," no longer seems so noble. We aren't as wise as we believed. We aren't as put together. We aren't as in control. The truth is, we are a mess, a small, selfish mess. Our selfishness had been hidden, but no more. Now we see it, ugly as it is. Our self-love is no longer composed or spiritually proud. Now, our self-love throws a temper tantrum, like a little kid screaming because he lost a piece of candy. It seems silly that exposing our selfishness should unravel us so violently, but the exposure inflicts a brutal torment.

Everything is a mess. Our self-love is in agony, but along with the pain, our self-love is also angry for being shown up as weak. Our self-love is chaotic, always moving, unwilling to receive any peace or rest. We keep searching to find another corner to hide in. When we have been forced to see how foolish and rebellious we truly are, the ugliness is despicable. Job knew this: "What I feared has come upon me; what I dreaded has happened to me." What our selfishness fears most—being pushed into the open—is exactly the necessary tool to destroy the false self's stranglehold on our heart.

If selfishness is dead, then there is no need for God to make his cuts. Only the parts of our self-love that are still breathing require God's surgery. So, odd as it might seem, what you needed was for your selfishness to be blatant, to be so unmasked that every bit of its grotesqueness showed. Your self-love needed to be so pummeled that the false self would wince and yelp at the slightest touch. This harsh assault was indispensable. But now, now that all the painful work is done, the easier part comes. All you have to do is to be still, willing to see your self-love with no masks, no lies, no illusions. As soon as you take that hard look, your self-love will be as good as gone.

You want to know how to make the pain go away. But you don't need the pain to go away. You need to die. Don't go running off after a quick fix. Let death come.

Be careful, though, even as you surrender to God's way of death, killing your selfishness. Don't let a false spiritual martyrdom take root in your heart. This is another way to allow our big sense of self to stay alive. Instead, open yourself fully to God. Keep it simple. Commit yourself to embrace God's affliction. Allow yourself to die.

Don't misunderstand me. You can't flex your muscles and make this self-death come. The more you try to "make it happen," the more painful it will be. God is wrenching this very kind of self-effort from you. Give in. Let yourself feel how worn out and exhausted you are. If you do, God's work will go much quicker. Of course, it is painful. And, try as we might, we cannot relieve the pain. Only God can.

Don't ask for some way out. Don't ask for a quick fix. However, don't ask for this death from God either. If you ask for the death, you are being impatient. And if you ask for a quick fix, you are just making your suffering stretch out much longer. Sit still. Let it go, and leave it in God's hands. Confess all your self-absorption to God; take it to him. Don't confess as a way of relief, just as a way of humbly submitting.

Even me, as your guide—don't look to me to save you. God is using me to bring you to death. That's what I am—one of God's death tools. Since that is true, it's okay if you think I am cruel or uncaring toward you, without any mercy, tired of you and your struggles. It's not true, God knows. In the strange way God works, I will actually be able to help you more if you think I have no compassion for you. My seeming harshness will do you more good than if I were sprinting to help you, full of kind words and warm affection. Remember, the real question isn't how you can hang onto life. The real question is how you can lose it all, how you can die.

To a Deceived Sufferer

Dear friend,

Be careful. There is something very hidden, very deceptive, in your suffering. It's lurking and waiting. Through this hard experience, you are convinced you are fully committed to God, wanting only God and God's way. The truth is, though, if you peer deep in your soul you will discover lots of self and not much of God.

You have stirred up all the trouble you are facing. It's true. You *do* want God to be seen. But not for *God's* sake. It's for **your** sake. You intend to use your distressing situation as a showcase to flaunt how fabulous you are, how impressively (how faithfully, how spiritually) you hold up under suffering. You are infatuated with yourself.

All this God-text is a ruse, another way of allowing yourself to be consumed with *you*. If you really want something profound and rich to emerge from the unearthing of your weaknesses, then don't cave in to either self-focused temptation: don't ignore your hard circumstances *and* don't highlight them. Don't push your troubles under the rug, hypocritically pretending you don't notice pain and making yourself appear better than you are. But, on the other hand, don't condemn yourself for buckling under the distress. The pain hurts. Admit it. Openly. To God. Quietly bend your will to God's, particularly in the things you don't understand.

In all of this, rest. Remain at peace. If you want what God wants, this one is easy: remember God always wants peace for you, always. No matter the circumstance. When rebellious sinners awake to repentance, what do they find? Peace. For a sinner, the suffering becomes a peaceful suffering with comfort mixed in. Do you remember the verse that used to give you much joy? I'm talking about the Scripture that says God did not speak in all the noise and confusion. Instead, God spoke in a gentle whisper.

Be at peace. Listen for the whisper.

To a Friend Who has Suffered Too Much

Dear suffering friend,

I feel sadness for the harsh suffering and sickness your dear friend is facing. And, remember, it isn't only your friend who is suffering. I feel sadness for the pain taken on by every true friend (like you) that God has put in her life in order to be with her, to help her carry her suffering. Don't let her lose trust in God. God will allow suffering, for sure; but not too much. God controls the amount, and for every bit of pain God allows, he will give patience and courage to endure. There is no one else to turn to for this patient strength. Only God can give the amounts of suffering we need (yes, need). Only God can give us the patient strength we depend on. God loves to provide for us when the situation is desperate. As God sees it, one of his jobs is to renew and to restore, to rejuvenate with grace.

Nobody—certainly not you or I—knows how to mix the precise amounts of suffering and strength. We don't even know when or where our suffering will come. We don't know how long suffering will afflict us. We have no idea what kind of grace will be required to hold us up under the pressure suffering carries.

Since there is so little we know, we are tempted to give up, to surrender to despair. It's like someone who has never seen the ocean. When they stand in the foamy tide for the very first time, with their back against a rock cliff, they see the surging waves, big waves. It is terrifying as the first wave rushes in. They are terrified that they will be swallowed up. But they won't be. Out in the water, a reef provides a buffer, and the strong wave cannot surge past because the sand of the ocean floor breaks the wave apart. Pain and suffering often rush at us like this wave, large enough to overwhelm us. But God marks the point the suffering cannot surge past. God breaks up our suffering just before the pain threatens to overwhelm us.

God tests his followers with ocean-like conditions. God stirs up the sea. God pushes huge waves toward us, waves that threaten to destroy us, drown us. However, God is always present with us, right there. And, standing beside us, God says to the waves, *you have come this far; you cannot go another inch.* Saint Paul said it this way to the Corinthians: "God is faithful; he will not let you be tempted beyond what you can bear."

From One Distressed Friend to Another

Dear friend,

Concerning our friend who is in trouble, I am praying that God will give him simplicity—and that this simplicity will bring him the peace he needs. This simplicity is vital for all of us. If we can jettison all the churning in our minds and if we can go deeper into our hearts, past all the external, surface issues that keep us constantly distracted, we will find ourselves plopped right in the middle of peace. The place that simple God-love invites us to is so different from the place toward which self-obsession pushes us. Simplicity picks us up (no work on our part) and sets us down in a wide-open meadow, full of sunshine and green grass. Jesus talked about the path to God as being straight and narrow—but the path isn't confining. God's path is wild and open and free. In this simple place, there is no guilt, no stifling restrictions. We have the peace that comes with being a child of God. And there is nothing—absolutely nothing—we need that God does not provide for us.

I'm not lecturing you. This is for me, too. I need to find peace this same way. Right now, my heart is suffering. However, it is my obsession with self that inflicts the pain.

If something is dead, it doesn't suffer. If we were dead, and if we truly saw our life as being wrapped up tight with a secure identity in Jesus, neither of us would suffer these sorts of pains in our spirit. The suffering in our body and the suffering in our soul would bother us little. But when our mind hits overdrive and we begin seeking relief or scheming to maneuver out of our uncomfortable situation, we actually pile on suffering and make our cross more painful than God intends. Agitated, we fight with God, swinging our clenched fists at God and especially the suffering he allows. This fight we will never win. Fighting God wears a person out. Self-protection wears a person out. We need to give up.

A cross that comes from God alone (not the suffering we inflict because of our wrangling) is somehow painful *and* peaceful at the same time. Strange. If we could welcome suffering without playing mental games, trying to scrutinize what we've done to deserve the suffering or what we could manipulate to avoid it, we would find peace.

However, if God's cross must force its way on us, it inflicts double the anguish. In fact, the inner skirmish where our soul fights against God is often more painful than the cross itself. Really, the cross isn't the main source of pain; fighting God— now, that hurts. If we can learn to recognize God's hand and if we can learn to stop pushing that hand away, we will find comfort in our affliction. We will find joy in the simple peace of trusting God, letting God send pain where he must. Nothing will shorten and soothe our pain more than surrendering to God.

Unfortunately, we like to bargain with God. We hope to avoid suffering altogether, but if we can't manage that, we at least hope to maneuver the amount of suffering God will allow. God doesn't bargain. God's cross arrives to confront our addiction to self-rule. Self-rule won't give up control easily, though, and it attempts to direct God's cross, telling God where to inflict pain and where to steer clear. With these power plays, our addictive self-rule demonstrates all the more how much work the cross has to do in us. Do you see that this is an insane merry-go-round? We need to get off the ride and let God do what's best. Our suffering will be much less if we stop fighting it.

The frightening reality is that we can resist so long that eventually God's crosses merely ricochet off our tough, self-protective shell. We will have grown so good at fighting them that they don't pierce us anymore. God save us from that!

The apostle Paul tells us that God loves a joyful giver. If this is true, God must take outrageous delight when we joyfully and with complete abandonment give him all of ourselves, when we willingly suffer his cross.

To a Friend Who Must Die

Dear friend,

Many are deceived. They think that God's work (helping them die to their self-absorption) is causing their miserable distress. The truth is that their suffering is not a result of self-absorption being killed but rather a signal that bits of self-absorption are still very much alive. Live bodies feel pain, not corpses.

The faster we can die to our self-infatuation (all of it), the less pain we will feel. If we don't push back against this spiritual dying, we won't feel any pain. If we would surrender to what God is doing, it would be so quick. The pain would be minimal. Our mind works against our surrendering, though. Our imagination runs off, exaggerating how horrible and terrifying this self-death will be. We argue and argue and keep arguing about how self-love actually offers much good, how it is appropriate at certain times, how we ought not take any of this death talk too far. Self fights and claws to the end, just the way you would expect a sick person might struggle to hold on, gasping for final breaths.

Our death is a death of body and soul, inside and outside. Death to our body will probably be off in the distance, but death to the self-absorption in our soul should be happening now. That way, if we have already surrendered our resistance to God and given up control of our life, when God's time comes to bring death to our body, it won't undo us. We will be at rest, trusting. Death will be like falling asleep. Anyone who is able to sleep like this, in peace, will experience true joy. That's what I hope for you—to experience much joy.

To an Inevitable Sufferer

Dear friend,

I know suffering. At times, crosses are all I know. My mind and body run over with suffering. Heaviness descends when the most joyful experience one knows is sadness or sorrow—that's where I am. However, we must carry our cross—even the heaviest one—in peace. Moving. Trusting. Resting. Even as you are under the crushing weight.

Having said that, I know that sometimes you just *can't* carry your cross. You can't even drag it. Sometimes, all we can do is fall down under its weight, overwhelmed and exhausted. That's okay. I know how wearisome this is, and I am praying for you. I pray that God would hold back as much suffering from you as possible. Suffering is like the "daily bread" we pray about in the Lord's Prayer. Only God knows how much we need, how much we can handle.

No matter how perplexing or dark, we must live in faith, trusting that our suffering brings us a kind of death that God knows we desperately need. We must move in confidence that God is knee-deep in our struggle. We don't see God's activity because God's kindness works undercover, secretly, hidden. Still, even without seeing, this is what we know: God provides as much help as we need to bear the testing he allows. This spiritual journey we are on is vital to our souls. It isn't child's play. Our life of faith requires the deepest kind of death.

Eighth Conversation
What Do I Need to Change?

All of our spiritual inquiry and wandering in search of wisdom often come down to a simple question: So what do I need to change? This question might surface from an unrelenting obsession with getting life right or a dogged clinging to the misguided notion that we can fix ourselves with one more spiritual adjustment. However, when we come to this straightforward question because we have received the care of a good spiritual guide, it is an immensely important, helpful q u e s t i o n .

When we inquire about change from a place free (mostly) of neurosis and a "fix-it" mentality, our question is humble. We have come to grips with our humanity and our sinfulness. We know we need help; we need grace. And so we ask, simply: What do we need to do next? We don't presume we know the answer. We just ask, and we trust we will receive a wise and kind reply.

Our question of what to change is also a bold question. We recognize that there are things to know, and then there are things to do. Spirituality (life) is not lived in theory. It is lived in the living. We don't want to merely talk about the life God has in store for us. We want to run into it. To do that, however, some pieces of our life need to be re-tooled. Knowing this, we move boldly, courageously, to ask what those things might be. The answers will stretch us. It's dangerous and risky to ask, open-handed, what we should change.

When this question—what do I need to change?—has been asked in a healthy way, a great deal of trust has been won. Before Fénelon's friends had the nerve to ask him this vulnerable question, they had already learned to trust Fénelon's voice and the heart behind the voice. They gave Fénelon authority in their lives. They asked questions even when they suspected the answers would be hard to hear. Perhaps this is a great watermark to judge whether you have found a true spiritual guide: have you humbled your heart to ask for the painful truth, and if you have, do you trust the answer you hear?

This is not to say that any human guide will guide us perfectly. Fénelon would be the first to challenge such blind trust. However, we must ask if our heart is truly open to being led. A guide cannot help us if we are not willing to be guided. And if we are unwilling to be guided, then that is the very first thing that must change.

Winn Collier

To a Friend Addicted to Spiritual Ambition

Dear friend,

I love that you speak openly and straightforwardly, telling me everything happening inside you. Never hesitate to write to me. Never hesitate to tell me anything, particularly anything you sense God wants you to share with me. I'm here for you.

I'm not the least bit surprised that you are feeling spiritual jealousy, having an overactive ambition to move up the Christian ladder and to be "more spiritual." So it's also no surprise that you have this strong craving to be friends with well-known people who are supposedly super-spiritual. These kinds of friendships and aspirations fit in quite well with our self-absorption. We are addicted to making ourselves look good, and our addiction is always hunting down more ways to feed the habit. These "spiritual" pursuits feed the addiction well, but are a big mistake. Don't feed those pursuits a bite more.

Stop trying so hard to become a great Christian (whatever that means). Stop trying to get close to high-powered Christians with big reputations. Stop it. If you want something to do, do this: cut off your self-absorbed addictions. Indulging yourself might feel good for a moment, but it's all a ruse. Instead, be humble. Instead of falling in love with yourself, love the fact that nobody knows your name. Love that nobody thinks much about who you are or about how super-spiritual you are. Don't look for the approval of the spiritual elite, worried about what they think or what they are doing. Look for God's approval. Live as if you have only one good eye, and use that one eye to always watch what God is doing and saying.

Of course, you are going to hear big stories about big people with big, perfect spiritual lives. People will talk and talk and talk, quite full of themselves. We can talk about spirituality all the time without ever being a single step closer to actually *being* spiritual. So, again, if you want something to do, do this: stop listening to the long, droning voices. Stop listening to the endless self-absorption. Just listen to God. Just God. In silence. See your narcissism for what it is—and chuck it. Give yourself to what is solid, to obedience and character, to virtue. Talk less than you act—and don't give a second thought to whether anyone sees your actions. It doesn't matter if they see.

What you need isn't all the big-name Christians or the most up-and-coming Christian books. God will teach you more than you could learn from other Christians, even the ones with amazing stories to tell. Even if you had every word that had ever been penned in any book in the world, you still wouldn't be able to learn from those pages what God wants to teach you directly, straight from his heart.

And I have to ask—why are you chasing after all this knowledge anyway? What we *need* is to recognize how much we *don't* know, to see how poor and desperate and helpless we truly are. Books and big-time teaching won't help with that. You don't need what they're pushing. You just need to know a few simple things: you need to know Jesus. And you need to know Jesus died on a cross. Pretty simple, huh? Saint Paul knew what he was talking about: "Knowledge puffs up while love builds up."

If this is true, then running after all this knowledge, thinking it will finally make you happy with who you are, is a waste. What you need instead is to learn to be contented with love. Just love.

Do you really think that the way to get rid of self-absorption, the way to learn to love God more, is by filling your head with more facts? *Really?* You already know more than you could ever possibly put to good use. You don't need to know more truth. What you **do** need, however, is to start obeying the truth you already have.

We are deeply deceived whenever we think our spirituality is progressing simply because our useless curiosity is being stimulated. We are running after new truths here and new truths there. It's all about getting what we want. It has nothing to do with loving God more. Just because your brain kicks in doesn't mean your heart is becoming more alive to God. So be humble. And stop looking to other people to give you what only God is able to (and desiring to) give you.

To a Friend Who Flinches at Correction

Dear friend,

I want so badly for you to have a rich inner peace. You do know, though, that there is only one way to find it, don't you? You must be deeply humbled.

Now, don't start kicking into high gear trying to figure out how to "get humble." You can't make yourself humble. True humility is something only God can work in you. And God doesn't work in the abstract. He chooses particular contexts, places of *living* flesh and blood, to nurture humility in our soil. You might not like it, but one of God's favorite contexts is having someone confront us with the wrong they see in our life. Through this discomfort, God allows us to see plain as day the weakness that we might have allowed to go unnoticed. Go ahead and get used to it—this is how God operates.

Do you want a test to know when you actually are humble? Here it is: whenever someone corrects your faults and whenever you see all the rank sickness in your heart—and you aren't surprised or offended by either—then you are humble. In that place, we don't have anything to prove, nothing to protest or protect. We assume that those correcting us must be right. Why wouldn't they be? We no longer cling to the delusion that we are so put-together. The correcting doesn't hurt because our identity and our well-being aren't tied up with being *good*, with being **right**. We know that we can't fix what is wrong with us, and so we give up on polishing our reputation. We feel the freedom of letting go.

When we see how much help we need and no longer commit to protecting the false image of ourselves, we expect others to see the truth about us. We aren't hiding. Even if the correction comes across harsh or insensitive, the words actually seem kinder than what we might actually deserve. If we wilt under another's rebuke, then the true culprit has been spotted. Our flinching at correction is worse than any of the faults that are being uncovered.

Even when you rebel against this correction, don't despair or beat yourself up. Your rebellion is actually serving as your friend, showing you how desperately you need to surrender to this painful process. The rebuke obviously touched a sore spot, a tender, sick place that might have stayed hidden if the knife hadn't pierced deep. The more pain we feel from the blade, the more certain we can be that there is something there that must be dug up.

I am struggling here. Please forgive me if my words have been too harsh. Don't allow yourself to doubt for one second how much I care for you. In fact, don't put too much stock in what I am saying. Look past my bumbling attempts to love you, and see God. God's hand is dealing you a painful blow, and he is just using my awkward hand to do it. If you feel pain from my words, then know that I have touched a sore spot. Lay down all the fighting and resisting. Lie down before God. If you will do this, you will find rest and peace in your heart—and it won't take long, I promise.

You are familiar with these words, aren't you? You are very good at giving this sort of advice to others. But it's hard when you are on the other end, isn't it? This is vital, though. This is life and death—you have to listen. If you will lie down like a restful child and trust how God will bring humility to you, and if you will surrender to how God is cutting away all the parts of yourself that you put so much confidence in, you will find amazing rest, stunning grace. You will drown in it.

I am praying that God will make you so small that you will hardly be seen at all. Then I pray that God **in you** will swell large.

To a Poisoned Soul

Dear friend,

What seems to be evil and destructive is transformed into something good and enlivening whenever it is received with a patient, restful trust in the power of God's love. However, what seems to be helpful is transformed into something dark and evil whenever we clutch it with an unrelenting grip, convinced we must have it.

You see, the actual object or circumstance or relationship we are starving for isn't the good. What we can cobble together for ourselves is never the good—good comes when we let go and wildly abandon ourselves to God. This very minute as you read, you are being tested to see if you believe what I'm saying is true. You are clinging to the rope and trying desperately to scratch and pull yourself to safety. Let go. Push off from the rock cliff, swing out wide—and just let go. Trust that God has you.

I would give anything to see your health returned to you. I don't want you to suffer. But more than not wanting you to suffer, I want you to be sick of the false loves you are so committed to. Whenever we are attached to protecting ourselves, we have drunk a lethal poison. It is a poison that will run through us, consuming us. This poison's venom is an obsession with self. It's deathly dangerous, and I am praying for you with all my heart.

To a Friend Overly Enamored with the Mind

Dear friend,

I am concerned for you. Your mind is too cluttered. You always try to figure things out. You live too much in your head. You fill the mental space so that there is no room for God. I find myself afraid for you because of your excessive addiction to brainpower. This addiction hinders your interior life, blocking silence and meditation. Your soul is so cluttered that God struggles to find opportunity to speak to you. You don't need to know more. You don't need to figure out more. What you need is to be humble. You need to be simpler, not more astute. You need to be open and straightforward with people, not always constantly working in your head and putting spin on what to say and when to say it.

Get out of your head. Come on out into the open where living is actually done. Tone down the mental franticness. Calm everything down. Stop trying to figure God out. Part of your problem is that the people who have influenced you the most are drab. They are aloof and dry to the bone. They trust their reason and intellect. They are critical and stuffy. These people are at odds with a deep inner life. With them, all you get is reasoning run wild. You get a dangerous brand of curiosity, drawing you away from the mystery and romance of grace and into the flatness of cold, calculated facts.

I have had time to study or read for four months. There is a time and a place for everything, and now isn't the time for study. We all agree that from time to time our body needs a fast to clear things out, right? Well, the mind needs a fast just as much.

If we are free, we will be immersed in joy. However, only the Son of God can make us free. And the Son has only one way of bringing us freedom and joy—he cuts away every rope strangling our heart. He cuts with a razor-sharp sword, slicing away every relationship and achievement that has become our idol. Until God does this cutting, freedom is only a word to us. But God won't let freedom stay in the abstract. He wants to get joy deep in you. So I'm hoping God will cut away. There's nothing to fear, though. What you will gain is far better than what you will lose. Just do what you know to do, and God will then be able to teach you more. Don't put confidence in your intellect. It has misled you too many times. I know how this is—my so-called intelligence has deceived me many times, too. Be simple. And grip this simple living (and thinking) tenaciously. All our brainpower will be short-lived, but God's truth will live forever. If God's truth shores up our trust, we stand in a solid place.

This is so important that I want to warn you one more time. Beware of philosophers and intellects who put their confidence in their mind. They will trip you up every time. You might think that you will be able to influence them, but they will influence you more. They like to talk around things and break down endless minutiae. None of it matters! And worse, they never actually come to the truth. They are gluttonous with curiosity. They gorge on knowledge, but it is never enough. It never leads anywhere. They consume a lot, but they never actually enjoy any of it. Do you remember Solomon, Israel's wisest king? He experienced vast knowledge, but in the end, he said it was vanity. It never satisfied any of his deep longings.

We should dive into studying Scripture only under God's direction. Even then, we should treat the work the same as going to the corner market. We go, and we get only what we need on that trip. No more, no less. Also, we must use our mind prayerfully. We must ask God to help us reflect who he is, the perfect balance of truth and love.

This is the crux of the whole matter of learning how to properly use our minds: we can know truth only in proportion to how much we love. When knowledge is divorced from love, it really isn't knowledge at all. It's just facts, dead facts. If we love extravagantly and if we stay humble about truths we don't understand, we will be able to live in the vast love God has for us. (And, remember, God *is* Truth.) In this place, we know what philosophers are completely ignorant of. There is a knowledge that only the little children and the simple-minded are able to possess. It is, as the disciple Matthew says, a knowledge hidden from the wise and the shrewd. I hope you discover this kind of knowledge.

To a Friend with a Shut-down Heart

Dear friend,

As God shines his light into the deep crevices of your heart, God is making everything clear to you. No ambiguity. You know what grace, the incredible generosity and kindness of God, is asking you to do; but you resist. You are saying no to God. No wonder you are so distressed. You keep telling yourself there is no way you can do what God asks, and the more you give in to these lies, the more despair you take on.

Despair about yourself as much as you like. Despair about how weak you are. Despair about how sinful you are. Despair about how desperate and small you are. But never, never despair of God. God is immensely good. God has a power you have never imagined. And God's goodness and power will move for you, if you will just believe him, trust, and follow him. Whatever you can have faith to believe, God will do for you. Scripture says you could even tilt a mountain with faith. However, if your faith is empty and you don't believe God will do anything, then *nothing* is exactly what you will get. If that happens—nothing—you won't have anyone to blame but yourself; God is here offering everything to you.

Do you remember Mary? The most impossible thing was asked of her, to bring the Son of God into the world—as a virgin, no less! Mary didn't hesitate. Luke tells us she simply said, "Do what you will with me."

Open up your heart. Right now, it is closed up, shut down. It is limp and small; it's bad. It isn't just that you aren't able to do what God is asking of you. You don't even want to be able. You don't want your heart to awaken. You don't want your heart to begin to pound in your chest, growing large and igniting all kinds of life. In fact, you are afraid of what might happen if your heart ever opened wide. How can grace possibly find space to wiggle in when your heart is locked down so tight?

I'm not going to ask much of you. I know you couldn't bear it. So, only two things. First: Rest. Calm all the fear and anxiety, trusting that God will teach you what you need when you need it. Second: Don't listen to self, all the inner voices telling you to protect yourself and shut down your heart. Simply have the humility to give way to God with all this, to stop resisting him and holding on so tightly. Quietly take in what God is doing for you, and as you do, let God's peace move into you. Over time (and it will take time), you will find that God is doing everything in you that you need, opening your heart and stirring up faith. Everything that now seems so impossible, so out of reach—God will take care of it all.

Guiding and Being Guided

A Short Biography

Fénelon's story is that of a man on a spiritual journey, encouraged along the way by a number of spiritual mentors.[4] It is only appropriate then that Fénelon's most potent legacy among modern Christians is not as a theologian (though his theological work is substantial) or as a political force (as he is best known among the French public today), but rather as a friend, a spiritual guide.

Born in 1651 into French nobility, François de Salignac de La Mothe-Fénelon was a sickly child. His illness required that his early schooling happen at home, a context that presumably was more relational and organic than the more formal, traditional options for primary-level education. Fénelon had many wise voices nurture him through the years. Tronson, his spiritual guide during his seminary training, offered friendship, wisdom, and instruction. Tronson also indirectly introduced Fénelon to one of his most significant influences: Madame Guyon.

While the content (the *what*) of spiritual guidance is often given first billing, some of Fénelon's earliest ministry work pushed to the fore questions of what he considered to be the appropriate *way* of spiritual guidance. During the French persecution of the Huguenots, Fénelon resisted those in the church who promoted violent tactics and forced conversions. His work as director of a women's college that initiated religious converts reflected his concern that dialogue and freedom, rather than coercion, be the path for spiritual transformation. Fénelon could never be accused of being theologically wishy-washy, but he also believed that the work of God in the human soul is something deep, something only God can do.

Fénelon became something of a voice for the oppressed. He saw the inherent humanity of even the unconverted. James Davis, a Fénelon biographer, recounts how Fénelon was irritated by some of the Jesuits who, as Fénelon described them, spoke "of this world only in terms of fines and prisons and of the other world only in terms of the devil and hell."[5] This passion for human dignity must have influenced Fénelon's desire to speak up against another prevalent form of oppression, the subjugation of women. Fénelon used his personal influence and some of his public writing to promote the dignity of women and to encourage French society to provide women more educational opportunities. He held great delight in the beauty of the human person while at the same time held great distrust for the perversions of human power, be they religious or secular.

This distrust made Fénelon a subversive voice. His family's nobility and loyalty to the French monarchy, as well as his own extensive education, made him a member of the French elite. However, he didn't pander to power. Fénelon's commitment to conviction and integrity made life dicey when he was named as a tutor to Louis XIV's heir and grandson. Fénelon had written a book for his young pupil called *Telamachus*, a novel that contained straightforward messages, rebuking war and promoting the idea that a king was to serve his subjects rather than vice versa. This was a dangerous, bold move. Apparently, Fénelon knew his role as a spiritual guide required boldness and truthfulness. Fénelon took seriously his call to help shape a young soul. He must have felt a seductive temptation to protect his prestige and prominence, keeping his unpopular opinions to himself and sticking to teaching the boy what the king wanted him to teach. But if he had, what sort of guide would he have been?

Fénelon's loyalty to truthfulness and to his spiritual relationships resulted in his being tossed out of the king's court. In addition to his work in guiding the king's grandson, he also came to the aid of Madame Guyon, his own spiritual guide. For multiple reasons, Guyon had grown out of favor with the aristocracy as well as the church. However, Fénelon would not allow his mentor to be unjustly skewered. Even if it meant his losing power and comfort, Fénelon would not abandon his friends or his integrity.

Contemporary opinion was that Fénelon had been castigated, silenced, and relegated to a life of obscure ministry. Some modern opinion still holds this view. One current Fénelon translator went to a French monastery for research. The monastery's abbot struggled to understand how Fénelon could possibly hold this translator's interest, suggesting another more prominent Fénelon contemporary that would be more worthy of his time. However, it was from this quiet, obscure place that we received what many would consider to be Fénelon's greatest life work. For the years that followed, he continued to correspond with a number of friends still serving in the palace. These letters offered (and preserved) what Fénelon had been giving and receiving for the better portion of his life: spiritual friendship and guidance.

Acknowledgments

Acknowledgments

Every writer hopes for a good editor. I had a dandy this time. Working with Lil Copan was the best part of this project.

Fénelon's life and Fénelon's friendships teach us the importance of connecting with wiser spiritual guides. God has provided me several during different life seasons. Pete Rice helped me stay sane in college. Nolan Jackson, though my time with him was short, walked with me in some hard places. Michael Cusick was my first spiritual director. I'm still looking for my second. Ken Edwards is as much a friend as a guide, but his wisdom is immense. He makes me want to live more passionately and love my family more wildly.

Of course, my first guides were my mom and dad. They always said their children were a gift to them. I think they are the gift.

One of the things I want most desperately is to see my sons' souls, to know their hearts and their passions, all the wonder God has crafted in them. I want to see them, delight in them, and then I want to guide them toward their unique place in the world. This hope of mine explains in part why I love Fénelon so much. He shows me that I *can* speak deep life into my sons' hearts.

My wife, Miska, is gifted as a spiritual guide. Seeing her work of spiritual direction, hearing her rich soul speak powerful words and pray powerful prayers, has given me a flesh-and-blood example of the impact of intimate spiritual guidance. Miska is an amazing woman, and I am crazy in love with her.

Notes

1. I have also pulled a small amount of material from Fénelon's *Christian Counsel*, also translated by Dodd in the same year.
2. While a couple of pieces are from another genre, almost all of the pieces here are well-attested letters.
3. Terry Tempest Williams, *An Unspoken Hunger: Stories from the Field* (New York: Vintage Books, 1994), 63–64.
4. A very good, concise introduction to Fénelon can be found in Robert J. Edmonson's translation of Fénelon's *Meditations on the Heart of God* (Brewster, MA: Paraclete Press, 1997). Bob was a tremendous help on this entire project.
5. James Herbert Davis Jr., *Fénelon* (Boston: Twayne Publishers, 1979), 18. Davis's work was a source for this biographical sketch.